Computing with
FORTRAN IV
A Practical Course

Donald M. Monro

Edward Arnold

First Published 1977
by Edward Arnold (Publishers) Ltd.,
41 Bedford Square, London WC1B 3DQ.

Reprinted 1978
Reprinted 1979 with minor corrections
Reprinted 1981

ISBN: 0 7131 2546 2

For Heather

Printed in Great Britain by The Pitman Press Ltd. Bath.

Preface

At Imperial College developments in the computing services made it possible to develop courses intended to give real experience in problem solving by computer to undergraduate students at a level unattainable by traditional programming courses. Having completed an introduction to computing using BASIC*, I turned to the ultimate objective of fluent FORTRAN and looked unsuccessfully for a suitable structured text before preparing the course which has grown into this book.

The traditional intensive FORTRAN course was defeated by lectures, coding forms, and poor turnaround, all of which divorced the student from his programming. By contrast I prefer to give only an introductory lecture and set the class loose on the facilities with assistance supplied and instructions to submit certain solutions by certain deadlines. The student prepares and runs his own programs and in my mind this is the important difference which does not require a timesharing service to make it work.

Almost every experienced programmer claims to be self-taught, and that is why I intend this book not as a teaching aid, but a learning aid. It is structured to the extent allowed by the nature of FORTRAN and endeavours to stress style and efficiency, while introducing many techniques and methods used in practice. The FORTRAN is essentially FORTRAN IV but some nonstandard features are too good to omit and some compilers are so restricted that the alternatives have to be outlined. I am well aware that a new standard FORTRAN is imminent but it will take some years to apply widely and we cannot wait for that. I take some care to point out common pitfalls and if some are overemphasized it may be because I once stumbled badly there myself.

Chapters 2 to 5 constitute a good grounding in practical application of FORTRAN to data processing and numerical computation. As in BASIC* there is a strong emphasis on numerical methods and this is taken to a more advanced level. This should not defeat the student aimed at science or engineering because I have tried to treat these as exercises in computing, not mathematics with the intention of making the computing interesting, even challenging.

*Monro, D. M., *Interactive Computing with BASIC, A First Course,* Edward Arnold, London (1974)

iii

I am grateful to Professor John Brown and Dr. D. Jones for allowing my approach to be developed on real students, and I am indebted to my colleagues J.M. Howl and P.R. Mason for helping to see the course through its first two years while protecting the students from my worst excesses. I have been fortunate in the help of Mary Mills who patiently typed her way through innumerable drafts, and Linden Rice has shown incredible tolerance in carefully preparing the final version in the face of many changes and delays.

1976   D. M. Monro
                                        Imperial College, London

Contents

1 Introduction

1 About FORTRAN

Those who invent acronyms have had more practice since the phrase
FORmula TRANslation was compressed into FORTRAN. It began as a
simpler, more restricted language but in its present form, known as
FORTRAN IV, it has settled down as the most common general purpose
vehicle for data processing and numerical calculation in science and
engineering. Many special purpose languages have sprung up ideally
suited to a bewildering variety of tasks, but none presents any
particular difficulty in learning after FORTRAN. Therefore FORTRAN
is the one computer language most worth knowing outside the commercial
field (where COBOL prevails).

Experience with FORTRAN has naturally brought an awareness of its
shortcomings and no effort is made here to conceal these. One
important consideration that reveals itself through trying to learn
it and later in helping others is that FORTRAN is not the ideal
language for a complete beginner because a large body of complex
rules applies to even the simplest program. In this connection a
special purpose language to mention here is BASIC because it is worth
learning first. BASIC enables beginners to assimilate the elementary
principles of programming with a minimum of fuss and is designed to
facilitate transition to the greater rigour of such languages as
FORTRAN. This course has been made general enough for any student
of FORTRAN with a suitable mathematical background, but it is
particularly suitable to follow BASIC.

2 About Computers

Man has invented many tools which strengthen his powers, and
computers are no exception because of their capability for automating
the repetitive calculations which earlier inventions have necessitated.
Every computer is a machine endowed with a repetoire of simple
instructions which it obeys blindly as a result of human guidance.
The job of organizing these instructions into a task for the machine
is called programming. The finished list of instructions is called
a program and is expressed on paper and to the machine in a programming
language, often FORTRAN. The computer has no way of knowing whether

the instructions given to it make sense or are what the programmer really intended. It interprets them quite literally and could easily get stuck repeating the same meaningless operation until stopped by human intervention or a timing circuit. The person who is trying to get a program to work correctly is capable of many mistakes but (usually) knows his intentions and can deduce what is going wrong. Much of the effort in computer programming is devoted to finding errors in the program.

The machine normally makes no errors but also exercises no judgement. Beginners are quick to blame the computer for making errors when they cannot find them themselves. Be warned, however, that in your first week you will lose count of your own errors but you may never run out of fingers for counting mistakes attributable to the machine itself.

Provided a computer is instructed properly it can outdistance in seconds or minutes a human lifetime of hand calculation. This is why computers have had a profound effect on a bewildered society. The effects are not always beneficial, particularly if a decision to "computerize" is taken in ignorance of the large overheads and highly specialized skills involved. But computers can add a million numbers a second and most can multiply nearly as rapidly with impressive precision. A computer can store thousands or tens of thousands of results in its memory and recall any one of them in a microsecond. It can be programmed to examine its results and make a decision and so can be given a superficial appearance of intelligence - but this intelligence originates with the human programmer and the computer's mistakes nearly always have the same origin.

A computer system is much more than a machine which does calculations. To be useful it must be surrounded by devices which feed it information and it must be given programs to guide it through its tasks. The person learning FORTRAN may communicate through a terminal with a keyboard for him to transmit information to the computer and a printer for its responses. Perhaps less fortunately he may have to use a "batch service" to which punched cards are submitted and from which the results are returned later.

A computer could have connected to it readers and punches for cards and paper tape, magnetic tape transports, lineprinters, and magnetic disk storage. All these devices provide for input (to the computer) and output (from the computer) of information. Each device has a "driver" program to control it, and there will be a supervisor for the drivers (and probably a program to monitor the supervisor). All these devices and programs make up a computer system before FORTRAN

Fig.1.1. A bewildering array of apparatus inhabits the Computer Room.

is taken into consideration and certainly before the "user" arrives to try his program provided of course that 'they' will let him get near it (Fig. 1).

The computer itself will not understand FORTRAN - the language it takes instructions from is a rather nasty series of numbers. Therefore a translation program or "compiler" is needed which takes a FORTRAN program and converts it to machine language. Because of the many facilities of FORTRAN and the need to check the grammar of a FORTRAN program, the compiler is quite a large program. Thus it takes many programs to run a FORTRAN program and the computer system that supports a FORTRAN programmer is an imposing collection of machinery ('hardware') and programs ('software'). The beginner is protected to an extent from any need for detailed knowledge of all this, but FORTRAN is a language that enables the expert to expand into many of the facilities of the system.

3 Interactive Computing and Time Sharing

Early computer systems were organized to deal with one program at a time, and programs were normally presented to the system in groups or 'batches' which the machine processed one after the other. The programmer submitted his program to a computing service which ran it for him and returned the result some time later. FORTRAN like any other language can be run in this way, and the majority of computing is still done in batches. The disadvantage of batch processing for small programs and for learning is that the 'turnaround' time is unlikely to be less than a few hours and is more likely to be measured in days.

An interactive computer system puts the programmer into direct communication with the computer, usually through a typewriter terminal Therefore the turnaround time for developing programs and finding and correcting errors is reduced to seconds. The program itself can be written so that the programmer gives it information while the computer is executing it and so he can control the steps of the calculation as it progresses. When FORTRAN is run in an interactive system, programs can be developed rapidly and tested and corrected from a terminal. The learning process is both shortened and made more thorough because the rapid response of the computer and the straightforward nature of the language work in the student's favour and encourage experimentation.

An interactive computer system can be in one of two modes of operation as seen by the programmer. These modes are 'program definition' and 'program execution' and are distinguished by

Programmer in control

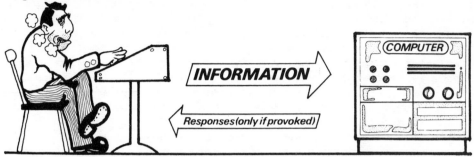

Definition Mode - *the programmer is entering, editing or correcting his program*

Computer in control

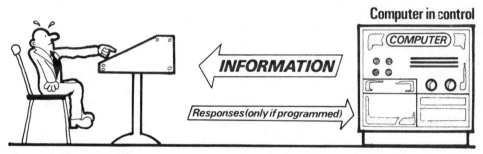

Execution Mode - *the computer is executing a program*

Fig.1.2. Timesharing divides into two modes of interaction.

whether the programmer or the computer is in control of events as in
Fig. 2. In the program definition mode the programmer will be
creating, editing and correcting his program and is himself in control.
The main flow of information is from the terminal to the computer and
any response by the computer is a result of the programmer's activities.
He can enter commands to the system, and the effect of some of these
commands is to transfer control to the computer. If this is done,
the system will change to execution mode and the user will be required
to respond only if the program has made specific provision for input
from the terminal. The main flow of information will be from the
computer to the terminal, and the programmer normally will regain
control when the program is finished, although he can stop execution
manually if necessary.

Time sharing is a means of making the resources of one computer
system serve the needs of many users at the same time. The computer
does not do several things at once, but it can be made to jump from
one task to another so rapidly that the individual user is not aware
of any long delays. Therefore interactive computing can be carried
out at many terminals 'simultaneously'. Large time sharing systems
can service a hundred or more terminals all using a variety of
languages to perform different operations, and also can do batch and
other work at the same time.

4 Batch Processing

The most likely form of computer service is the batch processing
arrangement which, although not ideal for learning, is efficient
for the production work which accounts for most computer usage. In
this kind of bureau, programs are submitted at a central site and are
fed to the computer in batches. Some time later, when the machine
has completed the batch and moved on to another, the printed results
are returned together with the program which will most often have to
be corrected and submitted again. The "turnaround" in a batch service
is at best a few hours and often overnight even for small jobs and
therefore the progress of a person learning FORTRAN can be badly
hampered. A service like this involves human intermediaries who
organize the input, sort the output and deal with hundreds of moaning
users. The user himself is likely to develop a somewhat jaded view
of the reception department. It should be remembered that
delays in processing are unlikely to be the fault of the unfortunates
who staff the reception area; many computers seem to have an uncanny
ability to develop sick headaches at the worst possible moment.

Some enlightened computer centres mitigate the delays of batch
processing by granting the user himself access to enough equipment to
run his own job, and this does tend to create satisfied customers.

Once the initial shock at the idea of allowing users to not only
see but *touch* equipment has passed, it is usually found that a well
organized "hands-on shop" in which people can read in their own cards
and tear off their own output is a success, if untidy at times.

   Almost all batch work is done from punched cards, and the deck of
cards that makes up a "job" must contain not only all of the FORTRAN
program, but also all of the necessary directions to the computer
system to make it run, and any data that the program is intended to
process. The directions, called "control cards" or "job control
language" vary widely between different computers as does the manner
of organization of the deck of cards. Typically control cards will
be needed to initiate translation or "compilation" of the original
source FORTRAN into machine language, to load this "compiled" program,
or "object code" into the computer, search the system libraries for
missing bits of program, and set it running, or "executing". A
complicated job may involve many more operations.

5 How to Use This Book

   The course is intended to be followed from the beginning in order,
doing as many problems as possible. It is necessary to have a means
of running FORTRAN programs on a computer, ideally by access to an
interactive system; if only batch processing is available it will
take longer. If possible a source of expert advice should be available, about FORTRAN because people who have made all the mistakes
already spot them more quickly (this is called "experience"), and
about the computer system which is likely to give more trouble than
the FORTRAN at first. The supplementary problems at the end of most
chapters are more demanding and should be regarded as optional.

   Each section should be read through before problems associated
with it are tried, and even the most tentative outline solution
to a problem will save time spent on the computer. It is tragic to
watch year after year the amount of time wasted in reading the
material for the first time and trying to think out the solutions at
the keyboard; the same people often claim to have had insufficient
access.

   A good introduction to practical computing is formed by Chapters
2 to 5, each of them requiring about ten hours of real work. If it
takes less, so much the better, but if it requires more then either
preparation and organization are inadequate or the level of the
course is inappropriate to the particular student's background and
interest.

Consideration must be given to students whom are recovering
from illness. en.

2 Calculations in Fortran

1 Introduction

A computing machine is directed by a series of instructions
telling it exactly what to do at each stage of a calculation; a set
of these instructions is called a program. Programming languages
are used to express instructions in a way which is independent of
the minute details of operation of the computer. FORTRAN IV is
called a "high level" language because it expresses calculations in
terms familiar to humans rather than machines. A FORTRAN program
uses common English terms and mathematical operations. However,
because the communication is with a computer, the instructions given
must be precise and no ambiguities can be allowed. Therefore the
grammar of FORTRAN, like any other computing language, is
constrained by a precise set of rules which control what grammatical
constructions or "syntax" the machine will "understand", i.e. accept
as valid instructions. These rules may make FORTRAN look
complicated at first, but they are there for good reasons, and
experience provides an easy fluency with the language because the
rules make sense. This is one of the reasons why FORTRAN is the
universal language of scientific calculation and has endured as such
for many years. In this chapter enough basic grammar and
construction is introduced to allow simple calculations to be
undertaken, although some of the material will have to be elaborated
on later.

A very simple example of a complete self-contained program serves
to introduce the language and point out some of the features of
construction. The following program calculates and prints the value
of π using the fact that $\tan(\pi/4) = 1.0$:

```
      PIE=4.0*ATAN(1.0)
      WRITE(6,20)PIE
   20 FORMAT(1X,F10.5)
      STOP
      END
```

Undoubtedly there will be things in the program that look familiar, and others that are partially self-explanatory. FORTRAN uses words of English and some recognizable mathematical notation, but it also has very strict rules of punctuation.

The program structure in FORTRAN is straightforward enough. Each line of the program is called a "statement" of FORTRAN, and some lines include statement numbers, as does statement 20 in this example. When a FORTRAN program is executed by a computer, the order of the statements dictates the order in which instructions given in the program are obeyed by the computer. So the given example is executed line by line just as one would read it; here the statement number itself does not affect the order.

This program contains several kinds of statements and other features which must all be understood before any program can be attempted.

The arithmetic statement

        PIE=4.0*ATAN(1.0)

may be recognised as a replacement or assignment statement for the variable PIE and * represents the multiplication operation. But why are the decimal points given explicitly in the constants 4.0 and 1.0? If they were left out the program would fail - some computers would reject it outright while others would produce the answer 0. Also important to a certain extent is the spelling of the variable PIE; were it called LIE instead a different result (3) would be produced by this statement.

The output statement

        WRITE(6,20)PIE

and its associated FORMAT

    20 FORMAT(1X,F10.5)

are involved with the printing of the result. But what does it all mean? In this particular example the value of PIE is written onto unit number 6 in a format of one space followed by the number right justified in the next 10 spaces with five places of decimals shown. This is not as complicated as it sounds and will be fully explained.

Fortunately the statements

    STOP

    END

are uncomplicated.

It is usual to consider programs in terms of flow diagrams which explain their construction.   A flow diagram of this example is shown in figure 2.1, which gives a graphical guide to the program steps.

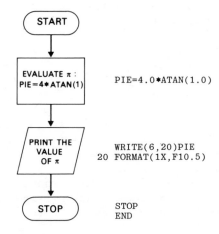

```
START

EVALUATE π :                    PIE=4.0*ATAN(1.0)
PIE=4*ATAN(1)

PRINT THE                  WRITE(6,20)PIE
VALUE                   20 FORMAT(1X,F10.5)
OF π

STOP                       STOP
                           END
```

Fig.2.1. Flow diagram of a simple FORTRAN program which evaluates and
prints the value of π.

It should be obvious from this example that the rules affecting numbers, variables, and arithmetic have to be outlined before any calculation can be attempted.   Some of the arrangements for input and output must also be understood, and so this chapter must attempt to convey a lot of detail which is absolutely essential to the FORTRAN language.*

---

*   Those learning FORTRAN on a time-sharing system could try the given example.

2 Constants, Variables and Arithmetic

Constants are numbers which are written explicitly in a FORTRAN program.   There are two kinds of constants in FORTRAN: reals and integers.   There are also two ways of writing real constants: with and without exponents.   An integer constant is simply a number, either positive or negative written without a decimal point.   The maximum allowed size of integers varies between computers.*

EXAMPLE: The following are integer constants

```
5
+1Ø24
-53
36ØØØØ    (not valid on a 16-bit machine)
```

Real constants are written with an explicit decimal point;   again the available range and the precision vary between computers although the range will always be much greater than the integer range.

EXAMPLE: The following are real constants

```
3.1416
5.Ø
+5.
63.
8.ØØ67
-1.
-2.7172845
```

The difference between the real constant 5. or 5.0 and the integer constant 5 can be very important in a FORTRAN program.   Indeed one of the commonest errors made in FORTRAN is the unintentional omission of the decimal point;   this can be rather a difficult error to trace.

Because the range of real values is large, real constants can also be written in an exponential form, such as

```
3.E1Ø
```

** For example on computers with 60 bit words the limits seldom cause problems since integers can be in the range $(-2^{59}+1) \le i \le (2^{59}-1)$ where i is the integer. With a 16 bit word the allowed range is usually $-32768 \le i \le 32767$ which can give trouble.

which means 3×10^{10}. The form of a real constant written in this way is

$y En$

where y is a real number written with a decimal point* and n is an integer exponent. Either can be signed.

EXAMPLE: The following are real constants written in exponential form

+3.E+1∅
−7.2E35
16.35E−4

FEATURE   :   CONSTANTS

Used to represent numeric values explicitly

FORTRAN	BASIC
A number, written with or without a decimal point	A number, written with or without a decimal point
Special Distinctions:	Special Distinctions:
Integer (written without a decimal point)	None
Real (written with a decimal point)	
Warning: the difference between 1. and 1 is often important	
Exponential Form	Exponential Form
$yEn = y \times 10^{n}$	$mEn = m \times 10^{n}$
y is a real number	m is any number
n is an integer number	n is an integer number

---

* Many individual compilers allow a real constant
          3E10
   i.e. omitting the decimal point. However, this is not recommended.

```
              FEATURE  :   VARIABLE NAMES

      Used to represent the value of a variable quantity
               in arithmetic calculations


          FORTRAN                        BASIC

Any alphanumeric combination     Any single letter or any
beginning with a letter and      single letter plus a single
having up to six characters      digit or any single letter
                                 plus a currency sign


Special distinctions:            Special distinctions:


Integer variables (normally      Variables with a currency
begin with I,J,K,L,M, or N).     sign are string variables
Real variables (normally
begin with A to H or O to Z)


Any variable name which has
special meaning to FORTRAN
is not allowed
```

The purpose of any calculation is to find unknown values from known ones and as in algebra, FORTRAN allows variable quantities to be given names.

Variables in FORTRAN can be given names consisting of several alphanumeric characters, and used sensibly these are an aid to clear programming since the name of a variable can help to explain its meaning. The standard rule is that as many as six characters can be used, although unfortunately this can vary upwards and downwards between computers. Generally speaking names of six characters or less are safe. The first character must be alphabetic, but the rest can be a mixture of numbers and letters.

EXAMPLE: The following are valid variable names of up to 6 characters

```
        X              ZERO
        Y9             J
        THETA          DALEKS
        KPRIME         P3264
```

The following are wrong

      3XY   (begins with a number)
      A$ (contains an illegal character)
      VAR73.   (contains an illegal character)

There are two types of variables: integers and reals. These are normally distinguished by their spelling, although it will be seen later that this can be over-ridden. An integer variable takes only integer values, and starts with the letters I, J, K, L, M or N. In the previous example KPRIME and J are integer variables (the rest are real).

EXAMPLE: The following are names of integer variables

      NUTS   L
      KPRIME   I73
      JOHN   MI5

Real variables begin with the other letters of the alphabet, A through H and O through Z. They can take values which are noninteger, i.e. those with decimal places.

EXAMPLE: The following are names of real variables

      OCTAL   DUMMY
      X   P3264
      FASTF   WIPE

In FORTRAN some names are illegal because they have another meaning in the language. For example, in the program given at the beginning of this chapter the words ATAN, WRITE, FORMAT, STOP and END all have a certain meaning in the language and so could not be used as variable names.

It is vital to appreciate the difference between reals and integers because the use of the wrong type in FORTRAN can cause trouble. Integers are exact whole numbers which carry no decimal places and for this reason are useful as counters and indicators. Reals, on the other hand carry decimal places and are therefore useful in calculations. Because the number of decimal places is limited, the results of real calculations are seldom exact. One would not use reals for counting, as will be seen.

EXERCISE: Classify the following as integer or real and variable
or constant. For example 5 is an integer constant.

154	E1Ø	METOO	B58
57.3	37	XI	1.
3.E1Ø	PRIME	1ØØØ	3Z

There are further special types of variables or constants which
are left to Chapter VI.

3 Expressions and Arithmetic

In FORTRAN variables and constants can be combined into what are
called arithmetic expressions involving the operations of addition,
subtraction, multiplication, division and exponentiation. For
example 3+4 is an expression in *integer mode* whose value is 7.
Priority relationships between the operations are defined so that
the meaning of any FORTRAN expression is unambiguous, and using
brackets the priorities can be adjusted to give the programmer
control over the evaluation of the expression. The available
operations are listed here in order or their priority.

high	( )	expressions in brackets
	**	exponentiation (a double asterisk)
	* or /	multiplication or division
low	+ or −	addition or subtraction

EXAMPLES:

4+5	integer sum, result 9
3.Ø*1.5	real product, result 4.5
1Ø/5	integer division, result 2
1.4142**2	real to an integer power, result approximatley 2.0

It is easily demonstrated that complicated expressions can have
ambiguous meaning. To a human the expression 4+5/7 could mean either
(4+5)/7 (addition done first) or 4+(5/7) (division done first). The
priority relationships between operations are used to make any
expression unambiguous to FORTRAN. In the evaluation of an
expression, the operations of highest priority are done first.
Therefore, exponentiation takes place earlier than multiplication or
division, and addition and subtraction are done last.

EXAMPLE: Consider the following expression which includes only integer constants

        3+5*2**4

When this is evaluated the order of events would be
                    visualise 2×2×2×2 = 16

        (i)   2**4 is calculated (result 16)
        (ii)   This result (16) is multiplied by 5 (result 80)
        (iii) 3 is added (result 83)

So the value of this expression is 83.

A careless programmer might have meant something quite different and written the expression in error. Possible intentions could have been

        3+(5*2)**4   (result 10003)
        (3+5)*2**4   (result 128)
or   (3+5*2)**4   (result 28561)

The use of brackets changes the order of calculation and so enables the programmer to make his intentions clear and explicit. Brackets can also make the expression easier to read, for example the same expression

        3+5*2**4

takes some thought to figure out, and could have been written more clearly as

        3+5*(2**4)
or   3+(5*(2**4))

for clarity. Note here that the brackets always must occur in pairs and in the last case this has meant two written together. Note also that the asterisk for multiplication can never be omitted. The expression 3+5(2**4) is incorrect and would be rejected. Multiple operands cannot occur, for example 4+-5, or 3*/5 are completely meaningless, and of course ** means exponentiation.*

---

*   4+(-5) would be accepted. This may appear paradoxical, but the + and - signs have two meanings, as part of a constant like (-5) which is their "monadic" meaning and as an operation of arithmetic as in 4+5, their "dyadic" meaning.

An expression involving multiple levels of exponentiation is
ambiguous if written without brackets, and so is not allowed. Thus

        3**4**5

is illegal. It must be written as

        3**(4**5)
or   (3**4)**5

whichever is intended.

   The expressions considered so far have included only integer
constants for clarity. They could also have included integer
variables; any expression invloving only integers (variables and/or
constants) is called an integer expression and is said to be in
"integer mode". A single integer quantity also counts as an
expression. The result of any integer operation is also an integer,
and this means that divisions involving integers cannot result in
decimal places. For example

        8/2   gives the result 4, as expected
        7/2   gives the integer result 3

Thus division of integers produces a "truncated" result, so that the
answer is the integer which would be obtained by stripping the
decimal places from the accurate result. This means that there is a
loss of precision in integer divisions, although truncation can be
used to advantage in certain circumstances as will be seen.

EXAMPLE: The following are integer expressions

        I
        I+J
        (I-5)**2
        J*3
        J+I/5   (when I is divided by 5 a truncation is likely)
        KPRIME+1

   Real expressions are those involving only real variables and/or
constants and are said to be in real mode; a single real quantity
is the simplest kind of real expression. The raising of a real
quantity to an integer power is a special case, which is said to be
in real mode. Thus

        A**(3+J)

is in fact a real expression. The precision of the results of a
real expression is preserved to the limits of the computer, and so
real quantities are used when decimal places are desirable.

For example the expression

(5.∅/3.∅)*3.∅

gives the result 5.0000..... or 4.9999..... which in its last
decimal places may not be exact, whereas the corresponding integer
expression.

(5/3)*3

has value 3 (exactly) because of truncation.

EXAMPLE: The following are real expressions

X   PHI**2
Y+Z   R/7.∅
FREQ*3.1416/PERIOD   A**B

If an expression involves both real and integer quantities it is
in "mixed mode" which is not allowed in FORTRAN IV. Note, however,
the special case of a real number raised to an integer power, which
is considered to be real.

EXAMPLE: The following expressions are of mixed mode, which is
undesirable.*

2*X   I+J**7.5
3+B   ANGLE/2

Again it is worth stressing the important difference between reals
and integers. An integer is used where an integer result is
necessary, such as in counting or removing decimal places. A real
expression is used when the result is to have decimal places of
precision. However in using reals precision can be lost. The value
of 0.1 + 0.1 + 0.1 is not likely to be exactly 0.3; it could be
0.3000001 or 0.2999999; this may not seem important yet but if a

---

* Nonstandard extensions to FORTRAN which do allow mixed mode expressions are fairly
   common, but even so the result of such an expression is governed by rules which vary
   between computers. The novice is well advised to avoid mixed mode altogether even if
   it is allowed.

FEATURE : ARITHMETIC EXPRESSIONS

The operations of arithmetic are performed according to the
hierarchy shown, which can be modified by the use of brackets

FORTRAN

BASIC

FORTRAN			BASIC
( )	expressions in brackets	high priority	( ) expressions in brackets
**	exponentiation		↑ exponentiation
* or /	multiplication or division		* or / multiplication or division
+ or −	addition or subtraction	low priority	+ or − addition or subtraction

Special distinctions: Special distinctions:

The mode of an expression is either   none
real, integer or mixed (which should
be avoided). A real expression to
an integer power is considered to be
in real mode.

FEATURE : ASSIGNMENT STATEMENTS

The usual means of calculation. An *expression* is
evaluated and the result replaces a named *variable*

FORTRAN

BASIC

called *arithmetic* statement   called *replacement* statement

Form: Form:
variable = expression   *line number* LET *variable = expression*

Special distinction: Special distinction:

The *expression* will produce a   none
result in either real or integer
mode. The replacement may imply
a conversion. If the *expression*
is real and the *variable* is
integer then a truncation occurs
in which the decimal places of
the result are discarded.

program is attempting to count to 0.3 in steps of 0.1 it is probably
not going to arrive. Reals are not useful for counting.

$$\boxed{\text{NEVER USE MIXED MODE}}$$

EXERCISE: Of what mode are the following expressions?

J   BETA
X**N   ANGLE/PERIOD
A+B-C   I**JOHN
I+3   X+5.Ø

EXERCISE: Which of the following expressions is illegal?

KPRIME**2.5   2.5**KPRIME
5Z   34.2*EXIT+7.Ø
A**B**2   Y+3
PHI/N   I-3J

EXERCISE: Suppose I=1, J=2, K=3, X=1.0, Y=2.0, Z=3.0.   What is the
value of each of the following expressions?

I+J*K   X+Y/Z
I+(J*K)   X+(Y/Z)
(I+J)*K   (X+Y)/Z
I+J/K   (X+Y)**Z
(I+J)/K   (X+Y)**J
(I+J)**Z   ((X+Y)**(J-Z))

4 Arithmetic Statements

All computing languages in common use have assignment statements,
which call for *expressions* to be evaluated and the result to replace
a *variable*. In FORTRAN this is called an arithmetic statement
(pronounced arithMETic; it is an adjective) and is of the form

$$variable \;=\; expression$$

for example

X=Y+46.Ø

which causes 46.0 to be added to the value of Y giving a real result,
and this replaces the value of X.   The arithmetic statement should
not be confused with a mathematical equation.   The statement

J=J+1

is an absurd mathematical proposition but a valid and very useful
statement of FORTRAN which has the effect of increasing the value of
the integer variable J by one (for counting among other things).

   The question of mode again affects the situation, but in a
straightforward way.   Not surprisingly, the expression on the right
hand side will generate a result which is either real or integer.
The variable on the left of the equals sign must also be one or the
other, but need not be the same as the expression.   Therefore a real
variable can be replaced by the result of an integer expression.
The variable remains real, and so the equals sign in the arithmetic
statement can imply a conversion from one mode to another.
Therefore the correct description of the statement

variable = *expression*

is that the *expression* is evaluated in its own mode and the result
is then converted to the mode of the *variable* if necessary, and
replaces it.

EXAMPLES:

I=I+5	integer expression I+5 replaces integer variable I, no conversion
X=4.0*PIE	real expression 4.0*PIE replaces real variable X, no conversion
BETA=J/5	integer expression J/5 (which may involve a truncation in the division operation) is evaluated and the result converted to real before it replaces real variable BETA
KPRIME=X**0.5	real expression X**0.5 replaces integer variable KPRIME after truncation of the result to an integer.

   This last example would usually result in a loss of decimal
places, or truncation.   For example, if X had value 2.0, then the

result of the real expression X**0.5 is$\sqrt{2}$ or 1.414....... which is then truncated to the integer value 1, before becoming the new value of KPRIME.

EXERCISE: Suppose I=1, J=2, K=3, X=1.0, Y=2.0, Z=3.0.   What is the result of each of the following arithmetic statements?

```
P=X+Y/Z              P=X+Y/Z**Y
P=J+I/K              M=(I**J)**K
M=I+J*K              P=X**(Y**Z)
P=Y/Z**J             P=Z**2/Y**2
M=X+Y/Z              M=Z**Y/Y**Y
```

5 Output of Simple Results—the WRITE and FORMAT statements

FORTRAN is organised around lines of input or output.   In a batch system a line of input is normally a computer card and a line of output usually appears on a lineprinter.   In the time-sharing environment input and output will be from a teletype or or similar device.   In either case the output is in the form of a printed line. A FORTRAN program can initiate input with a READ statement and output with a WRITE statement;   both terms are self-explanatory if it is remembered that the action taken is from the point of view of the computer.   For printed output, the WRITE statement specifies the variables to be written and there is an associated FORMAT statement which dictates the layout of the printed line.   A typical WRITE statement might be

```
WRITE(6,22)I,J,K
```

which asks that the three listed integer variables should be printed on unit number 6 according to FORMAT number 22.   In many computer systems unit 6 is the standard unit for printed output, but in some it could be different;   there may even be a means of assigning it.

Associated with this WRITE statement there must be a FORMAT state-ment which is given statement number 22.   The FORMAT statement is used to specify the explicit layout of the printed line, and does so by specifying "fields" of information.   This can actually appear anywhere in the program but it must be there to be referred to when the WRITE occurs.   The WRITE is an "executable statement", i.e. it causes an action to be taken and therefore its place in the program is important.   The FORMAT is "non-executable", and is there to be used by any WRITE statement which refers to it;   several WRITE statements could use the same FORMAT. A suitable FORMAT to accompany the above WRITE might be

//;3 instructions

22 FORMAT(1X,3I3)

which specifies that three integers are to be printed, each occupying three spaces, this is accomplished by the field specification 3I3. The line of output is to begin with a blank space, called for by the field specification 1X.

Taken together these two statements mean that the values of three variables I, J, and K are to be written to (i.e. printed on) unit number 6 according to the FORMAT with statement number 22. The FORMAT dictates that the printed line is to contain one space with the three integer variables following, each occupying three spaces.

The I or integer specification is only one of several possible types. The I specification

n I m

calls for n integers each occupying m spaces; in a FORMAT statement several I fields can be given with commas between. The printing takes place in one-to-one correspondence between the variables named in the WRITE statement and the fields specified in the FORMAT statement.

The X specification indicates blank spaces, so that a field

n X

calls for n blanks to appear in the printed line.

For example, the statements

WRITE(6,3Ø)I

and

3Ø FORMAT(3X,I2)

might appear in the same program and would produce the value of I printed in the fourth and fifth spaces of the output line, preceded by three blanks. It is entirely possible that variable I has too large a value for the field I2; any positive integer greater than 99 or a negative one less than -9 will not fit; in this situation the number will not appear. Depending on the computer system an error message could be issued, and the program could either abort or print asterisks in place of the offending number.

Each WRITE statement begins a new line of printed output. It is therefore impossible in FORTRAN to continue printing along the same line with more than one WRITE statement (although it is often possible to overprint lines, which is not quite the same thing).

EXAMPLE: Suppose the variables I=1, K=-53 and J=1024 are to be printed.   Then the statements

WRITE(6,43)I,K,J

with

43 FORMAT(1X,I4,1X,I3,I5)

will produce the printed line:

    1 -53 1Ø24
. . . .

whereas the statements

WRITE(6,43)I
WRITE(6,43)J
WRITE(6,43)K

in a program with the same FORMAT would produce the output on separate lines, as

    1
. . . . .

 1Ø24
. . . . .

   -53
. . . . .

If there are too many numbers listed in the WRITE statement for the number of fields in the FORMAT, then the FORMAT is repeated on successive new lines until all the numbers have been printed.

EXAMPLE: With the same values as above, the statements

WRITE(6,44)I,K,J

with

44 FORMAT(1X,I4)

would produce the printed lines

```
     1
. . . . .
    -53
. . . . .
  1Ø24
. . . . .
```

Specifications for real numbers are also available; for example the F specification which is a bit complicated. F stands for Fixed-point and is used to print real variables with the position of the decimal point fixed.

The statements

```
        WRITE(6,2Ø)X
    2Ø  FORMAT(1X,F1Ø.5)
```

cause variable X to have its value printed in spaces 2-11 of the output line, with five decimal places; the decimal point is printed.

In general the field

$$k\,F\,\ell.j$$

prints k real numbers in ℓ spaces each with j decimal places.

No conversion from real to integer or integer to real is implied by the FORMAT fields. Thus the variables listed in the WRITE statement must be in one-to-one correspondence according to type and position with the fields of the FORMAT; FORTRAN is strict on this point.

EXAMPLES: Suppose I=1, J=-53, K=1024, X=1.5, Y=-36.73, Z=3.14159265. Then the statements

```
        WRITE(6,41)I,Z,J,K
    41  FORMAT(1X,I4,F1Ø.4,2I5)
```

would produce

```
     1     3.1416  -53 1Ø24
. . . . . . . . . . . . . . . . . . . . . . . .
```

The statements

```
        WRITE(6,42)J,Y,I,X,K,Z
    42  FORMAT(1X,I4,F7.2)
```

would produce

```
 -53 -36.73
. . . . . . . . . . .
    1   1.5∅
. . . . . . . . . . .
 1∅24   3.14
. . . . . . . . . . .
```

by repeating the FORMAT three times on new lines.

The statements

```
      WRITE(6,43)I,X
      WRITE(6,43)J,Y
   43 FORMAT(1X,I4,F7.2)
```

would produce

```
    1   1.5∅
. . . . . . . . . . .
 -53 -36.73
. . . . . . . . . . .
```

The statements

```
      WRITE(6,44)I,X,J,K
   44 FORMAT(1X,I1∅)
```

would result in an error condition because an attempt is made to print X which is real according to an I field specification.

> Special Note: Always begin output FORMATs with a space (1X) until further notice.   Where a line-printer is involved failure to do this will result in unpopularity.   Reason: lineprinters regard the first space as "carriage control" and have a nasty tendency to jump to a new page if something other than a blank occurs as the first space.   Trees are becoming scarce.

SUMMARY: The WRITE statement

> WRITE(n,m) *list*

causes a new line containing the variables names by *list*, separated
by commas, to be written (i.e. printed) on output unit n according
to FORMAT m which must occur somewhere in the program.   Items in
list can only be variable names, not expressions.

> m FORMAT(*specification*)

gives an exact layout for the printed line.   *The specification*
consists of a number of fields separated by commas which must give a
format in one-to-one correspondence with the variables named in *list*
according to type.   The same FORMAT can be used by several different
WRITE statements.   The *specification* may be longer than the *list*.
If the *specification* is shorter than the *list,* then the *specification*
is repeated on new lines of output until the *list* is satisfied.

  The available field types include

> k I ℓ

which gives k integer fields of ℓ spaces

> kFℓ.j

which gives k fixed-point fields for real variables of ℓ spaces with
j decimal places, and

> kX

which provides k blank spaces.

  A line of output should always begin with a blank.

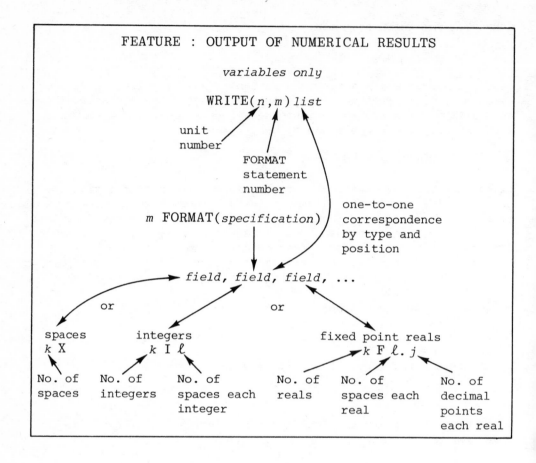

6 Structure of Simple Programs

As soon as the structure of a FORTRAN program is understood it will be possible to write and try some programs. As an example, suppose a sum of money PRINC has been invested at an interest rate of R% for N years. The gross yield is to be calculated, which is

GROSS=PRINC*(1.∅+R/1∅∅.∅)**N

FEATURE : STATEMENTS

The statements of any program are obeyed in order
unless the program dictates otherwise

FORTRAN   BASIC

statement number statement   *line number* statement
The *statement number* is optional   The *line number* is required

Note: In a time sharing system
line numbers may be required in
FORTRAN. These are NOT the same
as the *statement numbers*.

FEATURE : REMARKS OR COMMENTS

These should be included to explain a program

FORTRAN   BASIC

C *any remark or comment*   *line number* REM *any remark*
                                                            or comment
The C (for Comment) is the
first letter of a line

FEATURE : PROGRAM TERMINATION

Execution of a program finishes when a termination
statement is encountered

FORTRAN   BASIC

STOP   *line number* STOP

                                        or

                                        line number END

Execution of a FORTRAN program is   BASIC will terminate on
terminated by a STOP statement.   either statement.
STOP and END have different
functions in FORTRAN. The END   The END must be the last
must be the last statement of   statement of the program.
the program.

Suppose PRINC is 1000.0, R is 8.0%, and N is 5 years, then a FORTRAN program to provide the answer is

```
C A PROGRAM TO CALCULATE GROSS YIELD ON AN INVESTMENT
C FIRST ASSIGN VALUES TO PRINCIPAL, INTEREST, AND TERM
      PRINC=1000.0
      R=8.0
      N=5
C NOW CALCULATE THE YIELD
      GROSS=PRINC*(1.+R/100.0)**N
C FINALLY PRINT THE RESULTS
      WRITE(6,20)PRINC,R,N,GROSS
   20 FORMAT(1X,2F10.2,I5,F10.2)
      STOP
      END
```

FORTRAN programs like this are obeyed in the order that the statements appear (but remember that FORMAT is non-executable and could appear anywhere in the program). This program first assigns values to PRINC, R, and N, then calculates GROSS and finally prints PRINC, R, N, and GROSS before terminating. Different values of PRINC, R, and N at this stage can be used by changing lines of the program. The STOP statement indicates where the program is to terminate and the END statement is always the last statement of all - it identifies the end of the written program and must always be present. Fig. 2.2 is a flow diagram of this program. It is good practice always to draw a flow diagram; few programs are as simple as this one and these diagrams are an aid to programming and understanding. That is to say, they are helpful in both the synthesis and analysis of programs.

The FORMAT statement in this program is the only one to have a statement number, in this case 20. It should be obvious that this is necessary to make the connection with the WRITE statement. In FORTRAN statement numbers are usually given only where necessary although there is no rule against giving every statement a number.

This program also includes a number of lines of comments which provide explanatory remarks. A comment line begins with the letter C and is then followed by any remark or comment.

To get a program into the computer it must be entered in some form. The arrangements are different in Batch and Time Sharing systems.

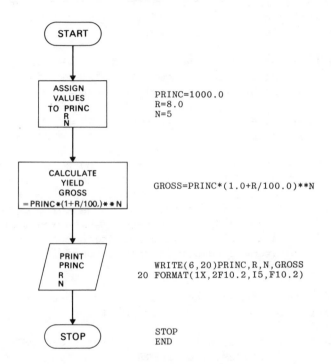

Fig.2.2. Flow diagram of a program which calculates the gross return
on an investment.

(a) Batch

Input to a batch system is usually in the form of cards. As well as the FORTRAN program a certain number of control cards will be necessary to identify the "job" and instruct the FORTRAN compiler to process the program. The form of control cards varies widely and so local information will be required. The FORTRAN program itself is punched on cards in a layout which is standard. Figure 2.3 shows computer cards with three lines of the example punched in them. The card is divided into 80 columns which are used as follows:

Column 1 - if a C is punched in column 1 the entire card is regarded as a comment and whatever follows is not part of the executable program.

Columns 1-5 - are used for statement numbers which are punched anywhere in these columns, if they exist.

Column 6 - is reserved for the special purpose of *continuations*. Occasionally a statement becomes too long for one card and it can be continued on a second card by punching a 1 in column 6, on a third card with a 2, and so on up to ten cards (which would be rather unusual). If a numbered statement is continued, the statement number is only punched in the first card of the statement.

Therefore only numbers should be punched in columns 1-6 except for the letter C which may appear in column 1.

Columns 7-72 - are used for the statements of FORTRAN. Within the statement of FORTRAN blank spaces are ignored, meaning that the statement can be compressed or expanded as desired.

Columns 73-80 are not used by FORTRAN but could be used to identify or serialise the cards.

The FORTRAN program consists of a deck of cards in the correct order, with an END card always as the last one. The program is submitted to the batch service with the necessary control cards and the cards and printed output are returned.

(b)   Time Sharing

There are great advantages to time sharing, particularly when writing and testing small programs. The programmer can enter his

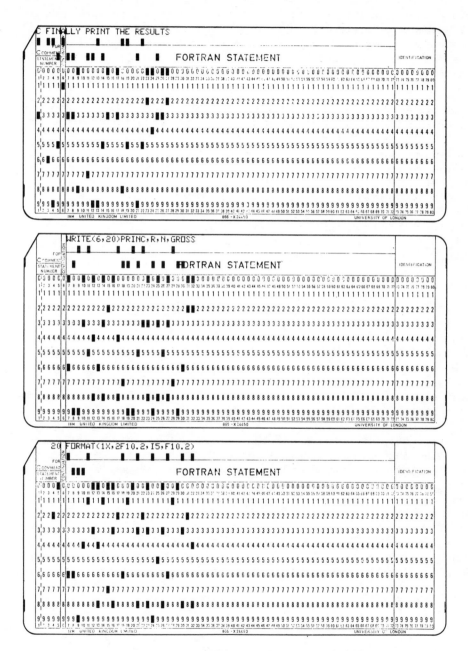

Fig.2.3. The layout of FORTRAN programs on punched cards.

FORTRAN program through a terminal, edit out his typing mistakes, try his program, and make corrections. All these operations involve only a few seconds delay. In a time sharing system line numbers will probably be required and these are not the same as the statement numbers - numbered statements have *both*. The following is the form taken by the example on a time sharing system:

```
00010C A PROGRAM TO CALCULATE RETURN ON AN INVESTMENT
00020C FIRST ASSIGN VALUES TO PRINCIPAL,INTEREST,AND TERM
00030 PRINC=1000.0
00040 R=8.0
00050 N=5
00060C NOW CALCULATE RETURN
00070 GROSS=PRINC*(1.0+R/100.0)**N
00080C FINALLY PRINT THE RESULTS
00090 WRITE(6,20)PRINC,R,N,GROSS
00100 20 FORMAT(1X,2F10.2,I5,F10.2)
00110 STOP
00120 END
```

In each FORTRAN statement, the line number is usually followed by a single blank space to signify the end of the line number. If a statement number is present, as in statement 20 (line 100) of the example, then it is also usually followed by a blank to indicate the end of the statement number. The FORTRAN statement then follows which can have as many blanks scattered through it as desired, meaning that the statement can be compressed or expanded to suit the programmer.

A comment is indicated by the letter C immediately following the line number, as shown. If a FORTRAN statement is too long for one line, then it may be continued on further lines by placing a *plus* sign immediately following the line number. If a numbered statement is continued, the number only appears in the first line of the statement.

In using time-sharing system knowledge of certain commands and other arrangements will be necessary, and since these vary widely between installations, this information must be obtained locally.

7 Problems

It is now possible to program and try some straightforward calculations in FORTRAN. Because of the amount of detail conveyed in this chapter, it is essential that practice in programming is undertaken. The following series of problems should all be solved before proceeding to the next section. There are as yet no arrangements which allow the input of data so the given values will have to be included in the program in each case. To change them, modify the program.

PROBLEM 2.1: A racing driver completes the Indianapolis 500 mile race in a particular time which is known in hours, minutes and seconds. Calculate his average speed in miles per hour.

Solution: This calculation lends itself to the use of real quantities. Suppose the elapsed time is XH hours, XM minutes, and XS seconds. Then the average speed is

$$\frac{500.0}{XH+XM/60.0+XS/3600.0}$$

NB: $\because D = S \times t \therefore \dfrac{D}{S}h = t$

in miles per hour. If the race takes 4 hours 36 minutes and 7 seconds, then a program to find the speed is

```
C DEFINE TIME IN HOURS, MINUTES, AND SECONDS
      XH=4.0
      XM=36.0
      XS=7.0
C CALCULATE THE DECIMAL TIME
      TIME=XH+XM/60.0+XS/3600.0
C AND THE AVERAGE SPEED
      SPEED=500.0/TIME
C NOW PRINT THE RESULTS
      WRITE(6,30)XH,XM,XS,TIME,SPEED
   30 FORMAT(1X,5F10.4)
      STOP
      END
```

which corresponds to the flow diagram of figure 2.4.

NB: 4H 36m 07s

$$4 + \frac{36}{60} + \frac{07}{3600} = 4 + 0.6 + 0.00194$$

$$= 4.601944 \, h$$

$$\therefore S = D\, t^{-1} = \frac{500}{4.601944}$$

$$= 108.65 \text{ mph ? or metres ?}$$

Rem: If Mtres then S & D = Km.

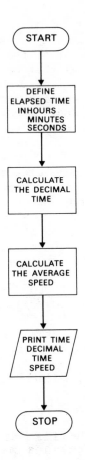

Fig.2.4. Flow diagram for the solution of Problem 2.1.

PROBLEM 2.2:   The amount returned after p currency units are invested for n investment periods at r% per period is

$$y = p(1+r/100)^n$$

as in the earlier example. This formula can be turned around in various ways. In writing these programs pay careful attention to the choice of variable type. Do not mix the mode of expressions.

(i)   Suppose the payments on an automobile costing 2000 currency units add up to 2400 units over a period of two years.   What is the true annual interest rate?   *(Answer 9.54%)*

(ii)   A man wishes to save a sum of money for the future.   If he needs 1000 units in 16 years, what single sum must he invest now at 6%, 8%, 10% per annum?   *(Answer 393.65 units at 6%)*

(iii)   How many full years will it take to at least double an investment at 6%, 8%, 10% per annum?   Find the answer by trial and error.   *(Answer 12 years at 6%)*

PROBLEM 2.3:   Back on the Indianapolis racetrack, find the time taken in hours, minutes, and seconds if the average speed is 180 m.p.h.   Helpful suggestion: here is an opportunity to use truncation.   The exact number of hours taken could be:

   HOURS=5ØØ.Ø/18Ø.Ø

but this must be truncated to the next lowest integer:

   IHOUR=HOURS

and to find the minutes, the noninteger part left over from the hours is used:

   X=IHOUR
   XMINS=(HOURS-X)*6Ø.Ø

and so on.   *(Answer 2 hours 46 minutes 40 seconds - you may get 39 seconds which is incorrect - why? - correct it)*

PROBLEM 2.4:   In the old British currency system there were 4 farthings to the penny, 12 pennies to the shilling, and 20 shillings to the pound.   How much old currency is represented by £4.278125?   *(Answer £4-5-6-3)*

8 Input of Numbers—the READ statement

For accepting the input of data while a program is running, FORTRAN uses the READ statement which is very similar to the WRITE statement:

   READ(n,m) *list*

This causes the computer to refer for input to unit *n* (which is often unit 5) where it will expect to be provided with values for the *list* of variables according to FORMAT *m*.   The statement

   m FORMAT(*specification*)

indicates exactly how the information will be laid out. *Specification*, as for the WRITE statement, consists of a number of fields in I, F, or X format which follows the *list* in respect of the type and position of data values.

   Again in these arrangements it is evident that FORTRAN is organised around lines of data;   each READ statement calls for a new line of information which in a batch system would probably be a computer card and in a time sharing environment would be a line typed into a terminal.   The meaning of the field specifications are as before, although there is an additional nuance to the F specification.   Therefore, the data is required to conform exactly to the given FORMAT, and so the value given to each variable in *list* must occupy exactly the stated space.   If it does not, the program will fail either by giving incorrect results or by being terminated.

EXAMPLE: The statements

          READ(5,2∅)I,J
       20 FORMAT(2I5)

are a request for values of the integer variables I and J to be taken from input unit 5.   The FORMAT requires that the value of I be right-justified to the fifth space of input and J to the tenth space.   FORTRAN will treat blank spaces in numerical fields as zeros, therefore the numbers 12 and 50 would be entered as

     12   5∅
. . . .

or as

     12   5
. . . .

Where the data misplaced, as

     12   5∅
. . . .

it would be interpreted as 120 and 5.   On punched cards it is easy to be sure that data is correctly aligned;   however on teletypes in a time sharing system great care must be taken over exact

spacing.   Figure 2.5 shows these numbers correctly punched on a
computer card.

Real numbers can be entered using the familiar F specification.
However, FORTRAN permits some flexibility in placing the decimal
point.   If the specification of a field is

$$F\ell.j$$

then the decimal point can be either omitted in which case the
computer places it before the last j digits, or it can be placed
explicitly anywhere in the field of ℓ spaces.   In this way the
specification actually can be over-ridden by the data by moving the
decimal point about within the field.   However, the number must still
fall entirely within the field of ℓ spaces. As another option
the number could be entered in exponential form - which also
has its own FORMAT described in Chapter 4.

EXAMPLE: The integer value 12 and the real value 3.14 are to be
   entered to a program which asks for them with the statements

        READ(5,15)I,X
     15 FORMAT(I5,F5.2)

This information could be entered with the decimal point of X
implied as:

     12   314
  . . . .

or with it given explicitly as either

     12 3.14
  . . . .

or

     123.14
  . . . .

These numbers are shown punched in cards in figure 2.6.

It is often wise to WRITE values out again after they have been
entered as a check that they are correct.   It is not necessary to
begin   lines of input with a space, although the X specification can
be used in input FORMATs.

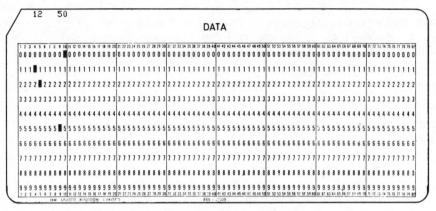

Fig.2.5. The integer values 12 and 50 punched correctly according
to the FORMAT(2I5).

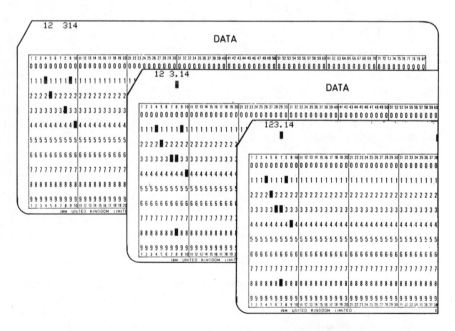

Fig.2.6. Three correct ways of presenting the integer value 12 and the
real value 3.14 according to the FORMAT(I5,F5.2).

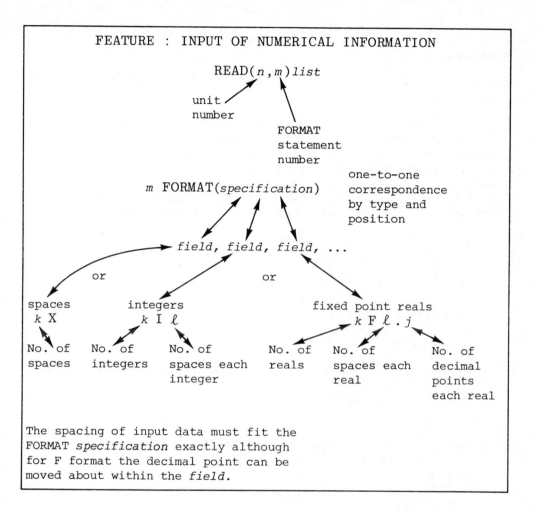

The spacing of input data must fit the
FORMAT *specification* exactly although
for F format the decimal point can be
moved about within the *field*.

9 Problems

PROBLEM 2.5:   Convert an angle given in degrees to degrees, minutes and seconds.

Solution: This problem illustrates the use of a READ statement to define the input angle. The fractional part can be obtained by truncation and converted to minutes and seconds. The angle will be read in as ANGL and converted to XDEG, XMIN and XSEC. A real variable FRAC is used to hold the minutes with its own fractional part and the integer variable I obtains truncated values by mode conversion in an arithmetic statement. A suitable program is:

```
C READ IN ANGLE IN DEGREES
      READ(5,21)ANGLE
   21 FORMAT(F1∅.5)
C PRINT IT OUT AGAIN
      WRITE(6,22)ANGLE
   22 FORMAT(1X,F1∅.5)
C CALCULATE DEGREES PART
      I=ANGL
      XDEG=I
C OBTAIN MINUTES AS FRACTIONAL PART OF DEGREES TIMES 6∅
      FRAC=6∅.*(ANGL-XDEG)
C TRUNCATE MINUTES
      I=FRAC
      XMIN=I
C OBTAIN SECONDS FROM FRACTIONAL PART OF MINUTES
      XSEC=FRAC-XMIN
C WRITE OUT THE RESULT
      WRITE(5,23)XDEG,I,XSEC
   22 FORMAT(1X,2F5.∅,F7.2)
      STOP
      END
```

A flow diagram of this program is given in figure 2.7. The program contains several deliberate errors. Find them. The only way to be absolutely sure is by running it with suitable test data. Do so.

PROBLEM 2.6:   Write a program to find the remainder when one integer number is divided by another.

EXAMPLE: 131/7=18+5/7. The remainder is 5.

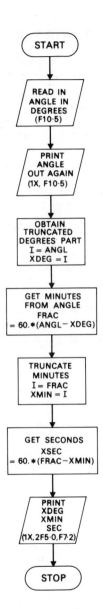

Fig.2.7. Flow diagram for the solution to Problem 2.5.

10 Repeating Calculations—the GO TO statement

To GO TO statement is a useful facility which allows the
programmer to dictate the order of events in the program, and using
it the programs written so far could be made to automatically repeat
themselves. Normally a FORTRAN program is followed by the computer
in the order of the statements one after another. However certain
kinds of statement can change this sequence, and one of these is the
GO TO statement. The form of it is

GO TO *statement number*

and it causes the execution of the program to jump to the given
statement number, which must appear somewhere in the program.

EXAMPLE: Suppose in Problem 2.5 it is necessary to repeat the
conversion of an angle from degrees to degrees, minutes and seconds
over and over again. This can be done by inserting a GO TO
statement in place of STOP, with a statement number added to the
destination, which is the READ statement. These would then become

```
C READ IN ANGLE IN DEGREES
   1Ø  READ(5,21)ANGLE
```

and

```
C WRITE OUT THE RESULT
      WRITE (5,23)XDEG,I,XSEC
   23 FORMAT(1X,2F5.Ø,F7.2)
      GO TO 1Ø
      END
```

The flow diagram of this program now incorporates a closed loop
or return path to the beginning, as in figure 2.8.

When a program such as the above containing an endless repetition
is run, in theory the computer could continue to execute it forever.
However in practice there are ways of terminating it. In a batch
environment the program will terminate itself when it runs out of
input data cards. On a time sharing system termination could be
accomplished by entering the word STOP in place of data, or by
striking a suitable key on the terminal to break into the program.
Try the following problems and in doing so, find out how to terminate
a program with an endless loop.

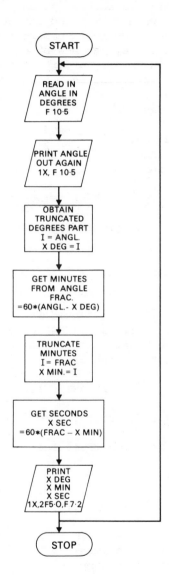

START

READ IN
ANGLE IN
DEGREES
F 10·5

PRINT ANGLE
OUT AGAIN
1X, F 10·5

OBTAIN
TRUNCATED
DEGREES PART
I = ANGL.
X DEG = I

GET MINUTES
FROM ANGLE
FRAC.
=60∗(ANGL.- X DEG)

TRUNCATE
MINUTES
I = FRAC
X MIN. = I

GET SECONDS
X SEC
=60∗(FRAC − X MIN)

PRINT
X DEG
X MIN
X SEC
1X,2F5·0,F 7·2

STOP

Fig.2.8.

PROBLEM 2.7:   In Problem 2.6 a program was written to find the remainder after integer division. Arrange a similar program which returns to the beginning to accept new data by means of a GO TO statement. By successive division and extraction of the remainders it is possible to convert decimal numbers to a different base; after successive division by the new base the remainders give the digits of the answer in reverse order. It should be obvious that this is a calculation involving only integers.

EXAMPLE: Find 131 to base 7.

$$131/7 = 18+5/7 \quad \text{Remainder} = 5$$
$$18/7 = 2+4/7 \quad \text{Remainder} = 4$$
$$2/7 = 0+2/7 \quad \text{Remainder} = 2$$

The answer is then 245, i.e. the remainders taken in reverse order.

Using the solution to this problem, convert

32767 to base 5
1000 to base 3
1024 to base 8

PROBLEM 2.8:   A polynomial ax^3+bx^2+cx+d is to be evaluated over a range of values of x.   Write a FORTRAN program to first read in a,b,c and d and then evaluate the polynomial as successive values of x are read in.   Plot a graph of

$$x^3-7.8x^2+18.5x-11.3$$

Approximately where are its roots?

Note: The most efficient way to evaluate a polynomial is to avoid powers of x which the computer evaluates only slowly, and to use instead a formula like

$$d+x(c+x(b+ax))$$

This requires only additions and multiplications which computers do very quickly.   This arrangement applies to any polynomial and can lead to great economy in computer time.

11 Built-in Functions

Most computing languages have a library of built-in functions which provide for the evaluation of often-used functions. FORTRAN is no exception and a very large number of such functions is available. Those listed in Table 1 are only a selection of many which can appear in a standard FORTRAN compiler; most computers will have these and others as well. It is worth reading the list carefully as there are some very useful facilities included.

EXAMPLE: Here is a program to find the square root of a number.

```
      READ(5,1Ø)X
  1Ø  FORMAT(F1Ø.5)
      Y=SQRT(X)
      WRITE(6,2Ø)Y
  2Ø  FORMAT(1X,F1Ø.5)
      STOP
      END
```

This program, when run, will request a value for the variable X from input unit 5, calculate its square root using the SQRT function, assign the result to Y, and finally print the answer on unit 6.

Functions can be freely included on the right hand side of any arithmetic statement, and as in the example above they operate on a quantity, called the *argument* of the function. *Arguments* can be expressions of any complexity including other functions. However restrictions about modes of expressions still apply. For example SQRT is a real function which takes a real argument, so that

$$SQRT(X)$$

calls for the square root of X to be found giving a real result. The example given at the beginning of this chapter calculated π using the fact that

$$\tan^{-1}(1.0) = \pi/4$$

The program used the real function ATAN of a real argument:

```
      PIE=4.Ø*ATAN(1.Ø)
      WRITE(6,2Ø)PIE
  20  FORMAT(1X,F1Ø.5)
      STOP
      END
```

NAME	MEANING
ABS(X)	Absolute value of X. (Real)
*ACOS(X)	Arccos(X), an angle $0 \leq a \leq \pi$ for which cos(a)=x. (Real)
AINT(X)	Integer part of X converted back to real. (Real)
ALOG(X)	Natural logarithm of X, $\log_e(X)$. (Real)
ALOG1Ø(X)	Logarithm of X to base 1Ø, $\log_{1\emptyset}(X)$. (Real)
AMAXØ(I,J,...)	Maximum of I,J,... converted to real. (Real)
AMAX1(X,Y,...)	Maximum of X,Y,... (Real)
AMINØ(I,J,...)	Minimum of I,J,... converted to real. (Real)
AMIN1(X,Y,...)	Minimum of X,Y,... (Real)
AMOD(X,Y)	Remainder of X/Y, i.e. $X-AINT(X/Y)*Y$. (Real)
*ASIN(X)	Arcsine(X), angle $-\pi/2 \leq a \leq \pi/2$ with sin(a)=X. (Real)
ATAN(X)	Arctangent(X), angle $-\pi/2 \lesssim a \lesssim \pi/2$ with tan(a)=X. (Real)
ATAN2(X,Y)	Arctangent(X/Y), i.e. $-\pi \lesssim a \lesssim \pi$ with tan(a)=X/Y. (Real)
COS(X)	Cosine of X, where X is in radians. (Real)
DIM(X,Y)	Positive difference $X-AMIN1(X,Y)$. (Real)
EXP(X)	Exponential function e^x. (Real)
FLOAT(I)	I converted to real. (Real)
IABS(I)	Absolute value of I. (Integer)
IDIM(I,J)	Positive difference $I-MIN\emptyset(I,J)$. (Integer)
IFIX(X)	X truncated to integer; the integer part of X. (Integer)
INT(X)	X truncated to integer; the integer part of X. (Integer)
ISIGN(I,J)	Transfer of sign; sign of J times $IABS(I)$. (Integer)
MAXØ(I,J...)	Maximum of I,J... (Integer)
MAX1(X,Y...)	Maximum of X,Y... converted to integer. (Integer)
MINØ(I,J...)	Minimum of I,J... (Integer)
MIN1(X,Y...)	Minimum of X,Y... converted to integer. (Integer)
MOD(I,J)	Remainder of I/J i.e. $I-I/J*J$. (Integer)
SIGN(X,Y)	Transfer of sign; (sign of Y)*ABS(X). (Real)
SIN(X)	Sine of X, where X is in radians. (Real)
SQRT(X)	Square root of X, where X must be positive. (Real)
*TAN(X)	Tangent of X, where X is in radians. (Real)
TANH(X)	Hyperbolic tangent of X; $(e^x-e^{-x})/(e^x+e^{-x})$. (Real)

Table 1.   Some of the more usual built-in functions of FORTRAN
All but those marked * are listed in the ANSI standard.
I and J are integer arguments;   X and Y are real arguments.

EXAMPLE: Some use has already been made of truncation to an integer,
for instance in problem 2.5.   Previously this has been accomplished
by mode conversion in an arithmetic statement.   The solution
contained statements

        I=FRAC
        XDEG=I

whose purpose was simply to strip the decimal places away from
FRAC.   Examining the list of functions, there is one called IFIX
which converts from real to integer mode, and another called FLOAT
which does the opposite.   Therefore the statement

        XDEG=IFIX(FRAC)
or
        XDEG=AINT(FRAC)

are equally useful replacements for the two arithmetic statements.
In this example FRAC is the argument of the function IFIX, and in
the second alternative the argument of FLOAT is IFIX(FRAC).

The program using these functions becomes:

```
 C READ IN ANGLE IN DEGREES
         READ(5,21)ANGLE
      21 FORMAT(F1Ø.5)
 C PRINT IT OUT AGAIN
         WRITE(6,22)ANGLE
      22 FORMAT(1X,F1Ø.5)
 C CALCULATE DEGREES PART
         XDEG=IFIX(ANGL)
 C OBTAIN MINUTES AS FRACTIONAL PART OF DEGREES TIMES 6Ø
         FRAC=6Ø.*(ANGL-XDEG)
         XMIN=IFIX(FRAC)
 C OBTAIN SECONDS FROM FRACTIONAL PART OF MINUTES
         XSEC=FRAC-XMIN
 C WRITE OUT THE RESULT
         WRITE(5,23)XDEG,I,XSEC
      23 FORMAT(1X,2F5.Ø,F7.2)
         STOP
         END
```

Still preserving the deliberate errors.

The *mode* of an argument (real or integer) is always important as
is the *type* (real or integer) of the function itself.   FLOAT is a
real function of an integer argument so that it can only appear in

expressions of real mode but its argument must be integer. This
provides a safe means of mixing together integer values into real
expressions. Conversely IFIX is an integer function of a real
argument; it results in truncation and conversion of its argument.
It turns out that FORTRAN also has the INT function which is
identical! Usually the first letter of a function name defines its
type but it does not define the nature of the arguments. Some
functions have multiple arguments which are separated by commas in
use; they may be a mixture of reals and integers. Examples are
ATAN2 with two real arguments and MOD with two integers. AMAX0 is a
real function of any number of integer arguments.

   In many cases obvious restrictions apply to the values that
arguments can take. SQRT, for example, should not be asked to find
the square root of a negative number, and ACOS(X) does not exist for
$|x|>1$.

PROBLEM 2.9: The library functions will usually give accuracy in
   their results which is close to the limits of the machine's
   capabilities. Because of these limits it is incapable of storing
   the exact result even if you try to supply it in your program.
   (a)   Use the ATAN function to find π. How accurately does your
   computer evaluate it, given that

$$\pi = 3.14159\ 26535\ 89793\ 23846$$

   (b) use the EXP function to find e. How accurately does your
   computer find it, given that

$$e = 2.71828\ 18284\ 59045\ 23536$$

PROBLEM 2.10: Write a program which, given the sides adjacent to
   the right angle of a triangle, finds the hypotenuse and the other
   two angles in degrees. Define the conversion factor from radians
   to degrees using the ATAN function.

```
+----------------------------------------------------------------------+
|                 FEATURE : BUILT-IN FUNCTIONS                         |
|                                                                      |
|           FORTRAN                              BASIC                 |
|                                                                      |
|   The supplied functions are        The supplied functions are      |
|   used as                           used as                         |
|                                                                      |
|       name(arguments)                   name(argument)              |
|                                                                      |
|   in arithmetic expressions of      in arithmetic expressions.      |
|   the correct mode (real or                                          |
|   integer).                         Argument is any expression.     |
|                                                                      |
|   The arguments are any                                              |
|   expressions of the correct                                         |
|   type (real or integer) for                                         |
|   the particular function.                                           |
|                                                                      |
|   The function may give a                                            |
|   result of type real or                                             |
|   integer.  The function name                                        |
|   is indicative of its type:                                         |
|   integer function names begin                                       |
|   with I,J,K,L,M, or N, real                                         |
|   function names begin with                                          |
|   A-H or O-Z.                                                        |
+----------------------------------------------------------------------+
```

12 Supplementary Problems

These problems, included at the end of each chapter, are intended to give extra practice in FORTRAN programming.

PROBLEM 2.11: Rewrite the solutions to problems 2.4 and 2.7 using functions wherever possible.

PROBLEM 2.12: December 31, 1899 was a Sunday. Write a program to find the day of the week for any date in the twentieth century. Leap years occur whenever the date is exactly divisible by 4, except that the exact centuries are only leap years if divisible by 400 (1900 was not, 2000 will be).

PROBLEM 2.13: The period T seconds of a pendulum of length ℓ metres for a small angle of swing is

$$T = 2\pi\sqrt{\ell/g}$$

where

$$g = 9.81 \text{ metres/sec}^2$$

(a) Write a program to find the period from the length.

(b) Write a program to find the length from the period.

PROBLEM 2.14: Write a program which finds the square root of a number x but which gives the answer $-\sqrt{x}$ if x is negative.

PROBLEM 2.15: Over the range $-1 \leqslant x \leqslant 1$, e^x can be approximated by a polynomial

$$e^x = 1.000045 + 1.000022\ x + 0.499199\ x^2$$
$$+ 0.166488\ x^3 + 0.043794\ x^4 + 0.008687\ x^5$$

which is one of the type known as Chebyshev polynomials. Compare this approximation with the EXP function and with the use of 6 terms of the series

$$e^x = 1 + x + \frac{x^2}{2} + \frac{x^3}{6} + \frac{x^4}{24} + \frac{x^5}{120} + \ldots$$

itself a polynomial. Use the efficient method of polynomial evaluation described in problem 2.8.

PROBLEM 2.16: Another method of finding e^x uses the continued fraction

$$e^x = 1 + \cfrac{x}{1 - \cfrac{x}{2 + \cfrac{x}{3 - \cfrac{x}{2 + \cfrac{x}{5 - \cfrac{x}{2 + \cfrac{x}{7 - \cfrac{x}{2 + \text{etc.} \ldots\ldots\ldots}}}}}}}}$$

which in practice has to stop somewhere because it would be programmed from the bottom up. Investigate the use of this formula as a means of finding e^x.

PROBLEM 2.17: The Chebyshev polynomial of Problem 2.15 was an example of an important method of approximation. Over a range $-1 \leqslant x \leqslant 1$ a function $f(x)$ can be approximated by

$$f(x) = \frac{C_0}{2} + C_1 T_1(x) + C_2 T_2(x) + \ldots + C_{N-1} T_{N-1}(x)$$

where $C_0, C_1, \ldots, C_{N-1}$ are Chebyshev coefficients and $T_1, T_2, \ldots, T_{N-1}$ are Chebyshev polynomials. It is known from theory that

$$T_0(x) = 1 \quad \text{and} \quad T_1(x) = x$$

and that higher order polynomials obey the recurrence

so that
$$T_{r+1}(x) = 2x T_r(x) - T_{r-1}(x)$$
$$T_2(x) = 2x^2 - 1, \quad T_3(x) = 4x^3 - 3x, \quad \text{etc.}$$

The Chebyshev coefficients are calculated from known values of $f(x)$ at the nonuniformly spaced values

$$x_k = \cos \left\{ \frac{(2k+1)\pi}{2N} \right\}, \quad k = 0, 1, \ldots, N-1$$

using the formula

$$C_n = \frac{2}{N} \sum_{k=0}^{N-1} f(x_k) \cos \left\{ \frac{(2k+1)n\pi}{2N} \right\}$$

Therefore a polynomial like the one given in Problem 2.15 can be obtained by deciding how many terms to use and calculating the Chebyshev coefficients. These are combined with the Chebyshev polynomials and by bringing together like powers of x a polynomial is obtained. The precision of the approximation is determined by the precision of the coefficients and the number of terms used.

Investigate the Chebyshev polynomial for calculating:

(i) e^x By suitable scaling a wider range than $-1 \leqslant x \leqslant 1$ can be achieved

(ii) Cos x Scale to cover the range $-\pi \leqslant x \leqslant \pi$.

3 Program Organization and Control

1 Introduction

Much of the power and all of the flexibility of computers derives from their ability to make decisions which alter the sequence of events in a computer program. One control statement has already been introduced - the GO TO statement which forces an unconditional transfer of control to a specified place in the program. In this chapter a number of control statements are presented which provide for conditional transfers, allowing decisions to be made in a program which change the order of execution.

The most useful is the IF statement, which occurs in two forms. These can examine either a logical or arithmetic proposition and take a decision based on the outcome. The logical IF statement was an innovation of FORTRAN IV and is now universally preferred by programmers for reasons which will become obvious. The arithmetic IF, an antique by comparison, is seldom used deliberately except by the unfortunate - a surprising number of FORTRAN compilers do not support the logical IF. Also introduced is the important "looping" facility of FORTRAN which allows parts of programs to be repeated a desired number of times, subject to certain rules and restrictions. There are also "assigned" and "computed" GO TO statements which are less often used.

2 Making Decisions—the logical IF statement

In FORTRAN it is possible to test relationships between expressions and take decisions as a result using the flexible and very convenient logical IF statement. The logical IF operates on the basis of what are called logical expressions, which for present purposes consist of *arithmetic expressions, relational operators,* and *logical operations.*

The simplest type of logical expressions would take the form:

arithmetic	*relational*	*arithmetic*
expression	*operator*	*expression*

with the two *expressions* of the same mode, i.e. either both real or
both integer.   The available operators are

.GT.	greater than
.LT.	less than
.EQ.	equal to
.GE.	greater than or equal to
.LE.	less than or equal to
.NE.	not equal to

written as shown.   The result of a logical expression is either
.TRUE. or .FALSE.

EXAMPLES:

I.GT.0   is .TRUE. if $I > 0$
                      or .FALSE. if $I \leq 0$

2.*THETA.LE.PIE   is .TRUE. if $2.*\text{THETA} \leq \text{PIE}$
                      or .FALSE. if $2.*\text{THETA} > \text{PIE}$

IFIX(X+Y).LT.J-1   is .TRUE. if the integer part of
                      (X+Y) is less than J-1, otherwise
                      .FALSE.

Logical expressions are incorporated in the logical IF statement:

IF(*logical expression*) *executable statement*

When the IF statement is reached, the *logical expression* is
evaluated.   If .TRUE. the *executable statement* is obeyed.   Often it
is a GO TO statement but it could be a READ or WRITE or almost any
executable statement.*   If the logical expression is .FALSE. the
given *executable statement* is not obeyed and the next statement
taken is the one following the IF statement.   In practice logical
IF statements are usually self-explanatory which is why they are
used so often in preference to the arithmetic form.

---

* It could be any executable statement except another IF or the DO statement.

EXAMPLES:

IF(B*B-4.Ø*A*C.LT.Ø.Ø) GO TO 5Ø

This is evidently the test of the discriminant b^2 - 4ac of a
quadratic form ax^2 + bx + c. If the discriminant is negative the
program will jump to statement 50, otherwise the next statement
will be the one that follows in sequence. Note the use of B*B
instead of B**2. It is more efficient to square a number this
way - computers do multiplication more rapidly than exponentiation.

IF(I.NE.J) WRITE(6,25)I,J

If I and J are not the same they are printed on unit 6. The
program then continues with the next statement in sequence.

IF(L.LT.Ø)M=M+1

If L is negative, M is incremented by one and the program then
carries on in sequence. Otherwise the program continues without
altering M.

FEATURE : DECISION MAKING

In both languages the principal facility for
decision making is an IF statement

FORTRAN

the logical IF

IF *logical   executable*
    expression   statement

If the *logical expression* is .TRUE.
the *executable statement* is obeyed.
Otherwise the next statement in
order follows.

BASIC

the IF ... THEN statement

line number IF *relational*   THEN *line number b*
                  expression

If the *relational expression* is TRUE, the program
jumps to *line number b*. Otherwise the next statement in order follows.

---

3 Example–Method of False Position–Flow Diagrams

Given the logical IF statement it is possible to prepare quite complicated procedures to do sophisticated calculations. In this section as an illustration a method for finding the roots of equations called the method of False Position will be developed into a FORTRAN program.

The method is very straightforward. Suppose a real distinct root of the equation

$$f(x) = 0$$

is sought. If there are two guesses of the root x_0 and x_1 which are known to be on opposite sides of it as in Fig. 3.1, then $f(x_0)$ and $f(x_1)$ will be of opposite sign. The method finds x_2, which is where the root would be if $f(x)$ were a straight line. Therefore on the secant joining $f(x_0)$ to $f(x_1)$ the new estimate is found as

$$x_2 = x_0 - \frac{x_0 - x_1}{f(x_0) - f(x_1)} f(x_0)$$

which is unlikely to be the correct answer, but it must be an improvement on whichever of x_0 and x_1 is on the same side of the root.

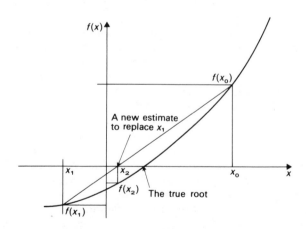

Fig.3.1. The method of False Position. x_0 and x_1 are initial estimates on opposite sides of the root. x_2 is a new estimate which in the illustration would replace x_1 because it is on the same side of the root.

Therefore x_2 can replace x_o if $f(x_o)$ has the same sign as $f(x_2)$, or x_2 can replace x_1 otherwise as in Fig. 3.1. The procedure can then repeat to find better and better estimates. A flow diagram such as Fig. 3.2 describes the procedure in outline.

The process of translating this procedure into a program begins with an elaboration of the details. The first question is how to decide which of x_o and x_1 is to be replaced by the new value x_2. This depends on the sign of $f(x_2)$. Using the SIGN function it is possible to test whether $f(x_o)$ is the same when the sign of $f(x_2)$ is transferred to it, i.e. if

$$\text{SIGN}(f(x_o), \ f(x_2)) \ .\text{EQ.} \quad f(x_o)$$

the signs are the same and x_2 replaces x_o. Otherwise x_2 replaces x_1. A similar approach can be used to decide if the initial guesses x_o and x_1 are correct so that $f(x_o)$ and $f(x_1)$ are of opposite sign.

Obviously the process of iteration which obtains successive improved values of x_2 is not intended to go on forever, so it remains to decide when the answer is good enough. The usual procedure is to examine how much the estimate has changed each time and base the decision on this. When a new value x_2 is calculated, the absolute value of change

$$\Delta = |x_2 - x_o| \qquad (\text{or} \quad |x_2 - x_1|)$$

is an estimate of the error in the root; a condition for stopping the iteration could be based on the size of this. But although this might be sensible for a small root, it will not suffice for large ones. For example a root near zero might be accepted if Δ is 10^{-5}, say, but it would be absurd to expect such a small change if the root were very large. For instance, if the root were at $x = 10^9$, then a Δ of 10^{-5} corresponds to an improved estimate which has changed by only one part in 10^{14} compared to the root, and this would probably be a ridiculously stringent stopping condition, if obtainable at all. To cover both situations, it is better to look for a certain proportion of error for large roots, i.e. the error is "normalized" to the size of the root. Accordingly it is decided in this program to accept the answer for a change Δ less than 10^{-5} if the root is apparently less than 1, and a change Δ of less than one part in 10^{-5} for a root which seems to be larger, i.e.

$$\left| \frac{\Delta}{x_2} \right| \lesssim 10^{-5}$$

The question "is the result acceptable?" is therefore elaborated in

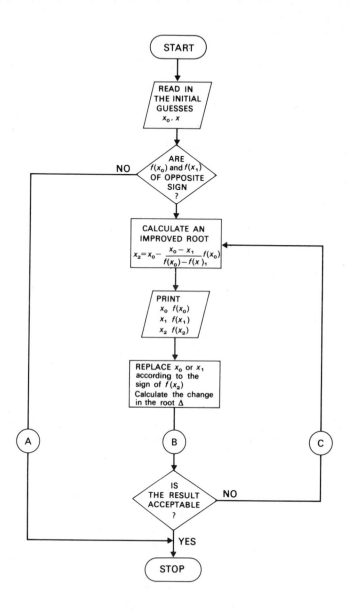

Fig.3.2. Flow diagram for the method of False Position. Circles A, B, and
C are connectors for later additions.

Fig. 3.3, and a flow diagram for the final program is shown in some detail in Fig. 3.4.

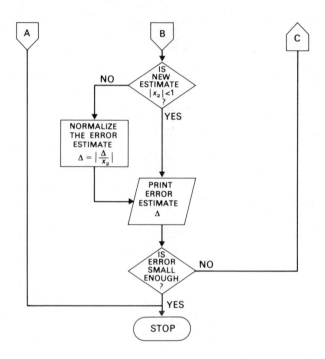

Fig.3.3. Elaboration of part of the flowchart for the method of False Position (Fig.3.2) to answer the question "is the result acceptable?"

   If the explanation of the process in words has been inadequate, the flow diagram should be worth an extra thousand or so to make up the deficiency;   this is their principal value.   It is usual to use the various flowchart shapes for the purposes shown in Fig. 3.5. In this text the shape for input or output is used instead of those for card or manual input because the programs could be intended for either batch or timesharing.   While many people could think through a program such as this one without flow diagrams, in practice most programs are more complicated and the effort of preparing flow diagrams most often results in less difficulty in the long run.

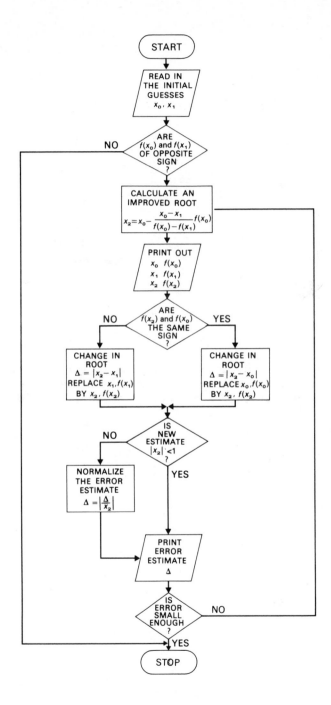

Fig.3.4. Detailed flow diagram for the method of False Position.

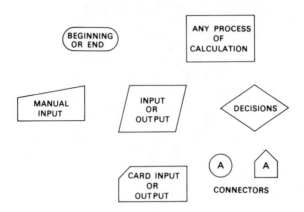

Fig.3.5. Conventional flow diagram symbols.

It remains to choose suitable variable names for this program and finally to write it. In FORTRAN the variable names can be chosen to at least partially explain their meaning. A choice could be

XØ   for x_0

X1   for x_1

X2   for x_2

FXØ   for $f(x_0)$

FX1   for $f(x_1)$

FX2   for $f(x_2)$

DELTA   for Δ

Suppose now that $f(x) = x^3 - 7.8x^2 + 18.5x - 11.3$, then the program comes out as:

```
C READ IN THE INITIAL GUESSES
      READ(5,1Ø)XØ,X1
   1Ø FORMAT(2F1Ø.5)
C CALCULATE FUNCTION VALUES AT INITIAL GUESS
      FXØ=((XØ-7.8)*XØ+18.5)*XØ-11.3
      FX1=((X1-7.8)*X1+18.5)*X1-11.3
C STOP IF FXØ AND FX1 ARE OF SAME SIGN
      IF(FXØ.EQ.SIGN(FXØ,FX1)) GO TO 7Ø
C CALCULATE AND PRINT THE NEW ESTIMATE
   2Ø X2=XØ-FXØ*(XØ-X1)/(FXØ-FX1)
      FX2=((X2-7.8)*X2+18.5)*X2-11.3
      WRITE(6,3Ø)XØ,FXØ,X1,FX1,X2,FX2
   3Ø FORMAT(1X,2F1Ø.5,5X,2F1Ø.5,5X,2F1Ø.5)
C NEW ESTIMATE REPLACES XØ OR X1 DEPENDING ON SIGN OF FX2
      IF(FXØ.NE.SIGN(FXØ,FX2))GO TO 40
      DELTA=ABS(X2-XØ)
      XØ=X2
      FXØ=FX2
      GO TO 5Ø
   4Ø DELTA=ABS(X2-X1)
      X1=X2
      FX1=FX2
C NORMALIZE THE CHANGE IF ABS(X2) GREATER THAN 1.Ø
   5Ø IF(ABS(X2).GT.1.Ø)DELTA=DELTA/ABS(X2)
      WRITE(6,6Ø)DELTA
   6Ø FORMAT(1X,F1Ø.6)
C REPEAT CALCULATION UNTIL DELTA IS SMALL ENOUGH
      IF(DELTA.GT.1.ØE-Ø5)GO TO 2Ø
   7Ø STOP
      END
```

EXERCISE: Try this program. Does it work? Can it be improved? No
   program is ever perfect.

SUMMARY: The steps in the preparation of this program have been:
  (i) A mathematical statement of the procedure
 (ii) An outline flowchart of the method
(iii) Elaboration of the details
 (iv) A detailed flowchart
  (v) A choice of variable names
 (vi) Translation into FORTRAN

Careful programmers follow similar steps in developing programs.
Although errors are always likely to occur there will be fewer if

the preparation has been careful. The most difficult part of
programming comes afterwards, when a program clearly does not work
and the errors in it have to be found.

4 More FORMAT Facilities—printing captions and repeating the specifications

All of the programs written so far have printed numerical results
without giving any printed explanations. A program is improved
immeasurably if messages can be printed as well as numbers. In a
FORMAT statement the H specification is available for defining
messages. The specification is

$$k \text{ H } message$$

and when encountered in a FORMAT the *message* is printed, which can
contain any combination of symbols as long as it is k characters
long. For example the statements

```
    WRITE(6,66)
 66 FORMAT(1X,12HHELLO SAILOR)
```

produce the message

```
    HELLO SAILOR
```

which is exactly 12 characters long, including the space. The
practice of starting lines with a blank is continued, but the
specification of a blank

```
    1H
    ...
```

is equivalent, so that FORMAT number 66 could be

```
 66 FORMAT(13H HELLO SAILOR)
```

Like any of the other specifications in FORMAT, the H can be used
mingled with others. The previous program could be improved by
printing messages in various places. Whenever input is desired in
a time sharing system a message should be printed saying what is
required and if necessary telling the FORMAT required; for example

```
    WRITE(6,5)
  5 FORMAT(36H TYPE IN TWO INITIAL GUESSES, 2F1Ø.5)
```

would assist in the method of False Position. Note that the
message includes the characters ",2F10.5." The character count *k*
in the specification *k*H must be exactly right to give a FORMAT whose
syntax is correct. In this example, if 37H had been specified the
FORMAT statement would lose its terminating bracket and so be wrong.
If 35H were given the meaningless specification 5 would confuse the
compiler.

   Similarly, in any program printed output is greatly improved by
the addition of captions, for example in the same program the FORMAT
at line 60 could be replaced by

   6∅ FORMAT(17H NORMALIZED ERROR, F1∅.6)

which prints an explanation of the output.

FEATURE : PRINTING CAPTIONS

FORTRAN	BASIC
WRITE(*m,n*)*list* *n* FORMAT(*specification*)	*line number* PRINT *quantities*
specification can include fields of H – conversion *k*H *message*, where message is any group of exactly *k* symbols, e.g.	*quantities* can include character strings enclosed in quotation marks, e.g. 1∅ PRINT "HELLO SAILOR"
35 FORMAT(13H HELLO SAILOR)	

   It will be recalled that in the situation where a READ or WRITE
statement comes to the end of the FORMAT *specification* before its
list of variables is satisfied, then the FORMAT is followed again
from the beginning on a new line of output. As will be seen, this
was not strictly a correct statement. Within a FORMAT, individual
fields or groups of fields can be repeated. In the program for the
method of False Position, one FORMAT, statement 30, contains several
fields which repeat

```
3Ø FORMAT(1X,2F1Ø.5,5X,2F1Ø.5,5X,2F1Ø.5)
```

This could be written

```
3Ø FORMAT(1X,3(2F1Ø.5,5X))
```

with the result that the bracketed fields are repeated 3 times; the
extra 5X is of no consequence. In any FORMAT, fields or groups of
fields can be bracketed and repeated any number of times; however,
FORTRAN will object if this exceeds the length of an input line (or
card) or an output line. Thus in the FORMAT one can have

$$k(fields)$$

as part of the specification. The bracketed part will be repeated
k times. In general there could be further embedded groups but
most computers will have some limit to the "depth" of embedding.*

   The truth can now be told about the repetition which occurs when
the *list* is unsatisfied. The entire FORMAT is repeated from the
beginning on a new line unless there are embedded bracketed groups.
If there are, the computer returns instead to the first embedded
left bracket. Therefore the statements

```
   WRITE(6,33)X,Y,P,Q,R,S
33 FORMAT(12H RESULTS ARE,(2X,2F8.3))
```

produce the message "RESULTS ARE" only once on the first printed
line with the values of X and Y following it on the same line. The
remaining four values are divided between the following two lines.
Every line has been started with a blank character.

FEATURE : REPEATING FORMATS

WRITE (m,n) *list*

n FORMAT $(specification)$

   Within *specification* groups of fields can be bracketed and
repeated as
$$k \ (fields)$$
so that the indicated *fields* are repeated k times.

   If the *list* is not completely satisfied when the end of the FORMAT
is reached, it is repeated on a new line or card, from the first
embedded set of brackets, or from the beginning if there are none.

---

* Often only two levels are allowed, i.e. FORMAT (...(...(...) ...) ...).

5 Convenient but Nonstandard FORMAT Facilities

Many compilers allow messages enclosed by special identifiers to be written into FORMAT statements without requiring the number of letters in the message to be counted and inserted. This saves the tedium of counting the symbols in H fields. Common "delimiters" used are quotation marks or asterisks. The earlier example could be

```
      WRITE(6,66)
   66 FORMAT(' HELLO SAILOR')
```

on an IBM/370 or

```
      WRITE(6,66)
   66 FORMAT(* HELLO SAILOR*)
```

on many CDC machines.

It is also possible on some machines to do without a FORMAT state- ment altogether. This will be appreciated by anyone working through this course on a timesharing system who will be very tired of the rigidity of input FORMATS. Some timesharing systems will allow Free-FORMAT input and output (which is not part of standard FORTRAN IV). Simply put

```
      READ, list   or possibly   READ*, list
```

for input. When the input is requested by the computer, it can be typed as numbers separated by blanks or commas. The one-to-one correspondence with the *list* according to type (real or integer) is still necessary; do not type in a real number without a decimal point.

For output, use

```
      PRINT, list   or possibly   PRINT*, list
```

and if messages are desired, it might be possible to include them in *list* with enclosing delimiters, either quotation marks or asterisks. If in doubt, try it.

PROBLEM 3.1.   Rewrite the solution of $x^3-7.8x^2+18.5x-11.3 = 0$ by the method of False Position to take advantage of these improved FORMAT facilities.   Give explanatory messages when asking for input on a timesharing system and print captions with output.   Print a message if the initial guesses are incorrect.   Run the program trying various combinations of initial guesses.   Develop a feeling for the rate at which the procedure converges towards its answer.   Can the answer be found for *any* choice of x_0, x_1 which are on opposite sides of the root?

PROBLEM 3.2.   The Newton-Raphson method will converge more rapidly than the method of False Position, *if* it converges.   This method requires only a single guess, x_1, and uses the slope of the function to predict an improved root.   Thus in Fig. 3.6,

$$x_2 = x_1 - \frac{f(x_1)}{f'(x_1)}$$

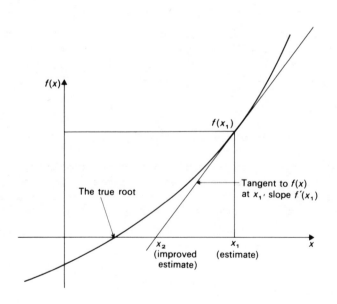

Fig.3.6. The Newton-Raphson iteration. The improved estimate x_2 is found using the slope of the function at the earlier estimate x_1.

Write a program to solve

$$x^3 - 7.8x^2 + 18.5x - 11.3 = 0$$

by this method. Compare its convergence with the method of False
Position, considering both the requirements of a suitable initial
choice and the rapidity of convergence.

6 Reals, Integers, and IF statements

  Before proceeding to further facilities of Fortran, it is useful
to consider more carefully some implications of the logical IF
statement as far as the type of expressions being compared are
concerned. In the comparison

> IF(*first expression* .EQ. *second expression*)*statement*

exact equality of the two *expressions* is required for the *statement*
to be executed. However with expressions involving real variables
and real arithmetic, exact equality is unlikely to be achieved
because although real arithmetic preserves as many digits of
significance as possible, it is not exact. The two statements

```
X=Ø.3
X=X+1.3
```

might not produce a result of exactly 1.6; it is apt to be something
like 1.59999..... which is not quite the same thing. Therefore a
statement like

```
IF(X.EQ.1.6)GO TO 2Ø
```

or even

```
IF(X.GE.1.6)GO TO 2Ø
```

could fail to behave as the programmer intended. Therefore as a
general rule it is unwise ever to expect exact equalities using reals.

  The first corollary of this general rule is that real variables
are unsuitable for counting. To state this in positive terms: always
use *integers* for counting. This is because integer variables always
have exact integer values and so will not present the programmer with
any nasty surprises in IF statements.

PROBLEM 3.3.   The speed of convergence of some numerical methods can
be improved by a procedure known as Aitken's delta-squared
extrapolation.   If three successive improved estimates of a
quantity are known, say x_1, x_2, x_3, then a further improvement is

$$z \simeq \frac{x_1 x_3 - x_2^2}{x_3 - 2x_2 + x_1}$$

This acceleration formula can easily be built into the method of
False Position (Problem 3.1).   The complication is that x_1, x_2,
and x_3 must be estimates from the same side of the root.   Integer
variables can be used to count how many estimates are available on
each side and so the extrapolation can be used at the right point.

Each time the Aitken formula is used, the improved estimate z
becomes x_1 for the next round.   Therefore the Aitken formula is
used after the first three False Position estimates (on a given
side of the root) and then after every further two False Position
estimates (on that side).   The whole procedure can be added to the
flow diagram of Fig. 3.4 as a simple elaboration, i.e. no major
change to the program structure is required.

Using the method of False Position incorporating Aitken's
extrapolation, solve

(i) $\ln(x) + 1 = 0$

(the answer is of course 1/e or 0.3679)

(ii) $x^3 - 3x^2 + 2.5x - 0.5 = 0$

(There are three, all real.   In finding the root
at $x=1.0$, the method should alternate between
sides.)

7 More Complicated Logical Expressions

Only the simplest logical expressions have so far been used in
logical IF statements.   In addition FORTRAN allows the use of three
logical operators in forming more complicated expressions: .NOT.,
.AND., and .OR.   They are used as:

	Logical expression a	Logical operator	Logical expression b	

Logical expression a	Operator	Logical expression b	Logical result
	·NOT·	·TRUE· ·FALSE·	·FALSE· ·TRUE·
·TRUE· ·TRUE· ·FALSE· ·FALSE·	·AND·	·TRUE· ·FALSE· ·TRUE· ·FALSE·	·TRUE· ·FALSE· ·FALSE· ·FALSE·
·TRUE· ·TRUE· ·FALSE· ·FALSE·	·OR·	·TRUE· ·FALSE· ·TRUE· ·FALSE·	·TRUE· ·TRUE· ·TRUE· ·FALSE·

Fig.3.7. Truth table for the logical operations of FORTRAN.
The .OR. is inclusive.

.NOT. *logical expression*
This "inverts" the result, i.e. if the *logical expression* were .TRUE. the .NOT. makes the result .FALSE. and vice versa.

logical expression .AND. *logical expression*
This is .TRUE. if both *logical expressions* are .TRUE., otherwise .FALSE.

logical expression .OR. *logical expression*
This is the "inclusive OR" and is .TRUE. if either or both of the *logical expressions* are .TRUE., otherwise .FALSE.

A truth table for these operators is given in Fig. 3.7. The rules for their application depend mainly on common sense. As before, the mode of an arithmetic expression is important with the relational operators .GT., .GE., .EQ., .LE., .LT., and .NE. but the result of a relational operation is either .TRUE. or .FALSE., i.e. it is no longer real or integer but logical. Logical mode is, in fact, a mode of FORTRAN. As might be expected, expressions operated on by .NOT., .AND., and .OR. must already be logical. Therefore a correct expression is one like

I.GT.J.OR.X.LE.3.14

whereas the following expression is doubly wrong because it mixes real, integer and logical modes:

A.AND.B.LT.75

Here, both .AND. and .LT. have been used improperly (assuming A and B are real; there is no reason up to this point to suppose they are not).

Logical expressions can be compounded, but then as with ordinary arithmetic, the meaning of expressions can be unclear unless brackets are used or the hierarchy is defined. For example, does the expression

MARK.GT.7.OR.LESLIE.EQ.5.AND.JOHN.LE.15

mean

(MARK.GT.7.OR.LESLIE.EQ.5).AND.(JOHN.LE.15)

```
FEATURE : LOGICAL EXPRESSIONS

             Used principally in IF statements
                    (but see Chapter 6)
```

FORTRAN	BASIC
logical logical logical *expression operator expression*	*arithmetic relational arithmetic* *expression operator expression*
The result is .TRUE. or .FALSE.	The result is TRUE or FALSE

The available *logical operators* are:

.NOT.   logical inversion

.AND.   logical multiplication

.OR.   logical addition

The available *relational operators* are:

>	greater than
>= or =>	greater or equal
=	equal to
<= or =<	less or equal
	less than

There are no restrictions on the *arithmetic expressions*.

Truth tables, Fig. 3.7

These *logical expressions* can be further *logical expressions* involving .NOT., .AND., .OR. or *relational expressions* of form:

arithmetic relational arithmetic *expression operator   expression*

The result is .TRUE. or .FALSE.

The *relational operators* are

.GT.   greater than

.GE.   greater or equal

.EQ.   equal to

.LE.   less or equal

.LT.   less than

.NE.   not equal

The *arithmetic expressions* must be of the same mode (real or integer).

The total hierarchy of FORTRAN expressions is given in the text.

or does it mean instead

$$(MARK.GT.7).OR.(LESLIE.EQ.5.AND.JOHN.LE.15)$$

which give different results in a situation such as MARK = 8,
LESLIE = 6, JOHN = 16.   It turns out that the second version is
correct.   The order of priority is:

highest	( )	expressions in brackets
	**	exponentiation
	*/	multiplication and division
	+-	addition and subtraction
	.GT., .GE., .EQ., .LE., .LT., .NE.	
	.NOT.	
	.AND.	
lowest	.OR.	

Examination of this table shows that .AND. is performed before .OR.
which explains the earlier expression.

PROBLEM 3.4.   Digital plotting machines are widely used to produce
   various forms of drawings, graphs, and other pictorial results.
   Most such machines can move their pens only in certain directions,
   usually as single steps in the X or Y direction or both.   A typical
   machine would move in one of the eight directions shown in Fig. 3.8.
   Smooth curves are made up of a very large number of single steps in
   these eight directions.
      Programs which control these devices have to be very efficient;
   although the algebra of pen motion lends itself to the use of
   trigonometric functions, these would be too slow in practice.
   Instead carefully organised logic and arithmetic is used involving
   the minimum of computation.

      (i)   Write a program without trigonometric functions which
   "encodes" the integer co-ordinates of the end points in Fig. 3.8
   into a number from 0 to 7.

      (ii)   Write a program without trigonometric functions which
   decodes a number from 0 to 7 into the integer co-ordinates of the
   end points in Fig. 3.8.

      (iii)   Write programs for rotation of the step direction:

given integer end co-ordinates calculate new ones from them
directly for rotations of 45° or 135° clockwise or anticlockwise.
The most efficient schemes would not use the encoding and
decoding method.

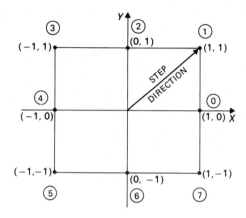

Fig.3.8. Digital drawing machines can move their pens in single steps
from the centre towards eight possible positions on the box. Programs
are desired to encode, decode, and rotate the direction of pen motion.

8 Looping with the IF statement

Closed loops occur in programs when the program contains a return path so that a part of the calculation is repeated. These loops can be unconditional, as with the GO TO statement, or conditional as in the method of False Position, when the loop was repeated until the error estimate became small. It is also possible to repeat a loop a fixed number of times by setting aside an integer variable to count through the loop.

Suppose a loop is to be repeated 10 times. Then an integer variable I could be used to count the repetitions, as in the flow diagram, Fig. 3.9. Before the loop I is set to 1, and then each time the end of the loop is reached another 1 is added to it. Therefore I takes the successive values 1, 2, 3 ... An IF statement at the end of the loop tests for completion, returning to the beginning of the loop until I is greater than 10. The required statements are:

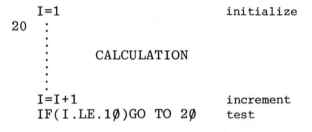

```
      I=1                          initialize
  20  :
      :
      :           CALCULATION
      :
      :
      I=I+1                        increment
      IF(I.LE.1Ø)GO TO 2Ø    test
```

Integer variables are used in preference to real ones for counting the repetitions in this kind of loop for a very good reason. With real variables one can never be absolutely sure that their value is exact even when working with apparently whole numbers. It is a good rule *never* to use real variables in any situation where the correct function of a program depends on their exact equality in an IF statement. This means, among other things, that loop counting should always be done using integers. If a sequence of real values is desired they can be obtained from an integer loop counter as in the following example.

EXAMPLE. A table of sines is to be calculated for the angles 0°, 10°, ..., 90°. The SIN function must therefore be called with a series of arguments (in radians)

$$0, \ \pi/18, \ 2\pi/18, \ ..., \ \pi/2$$

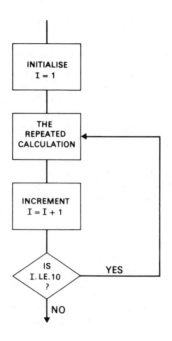

Fig.3.9. Organization of a counting loop repeated 10 times.

It would not be sensible to use a real variable to count because
it could fail on the ultimate test and not give the value $Sin(\pi/2)$.
Instead an integer variable ITHETA is used to count from 0 to 9
and the angle THETA in radians is derived from it as

THETA=FLOAT(ITHETA)*π/18.0

The same term $\pi/18$ occurs for every calculation and should be
removed from the loop for efficiency, so that it is calculated
only once rather than in the loop 10 times. Removing this kind
of invariant calculation from inside a loop can be an important
factor in improving the efficiency of a program. An accurate
value of π is obtained from the ATAN function. Therefore a
suitable program is

```
C PRINT A TABLE OF SINES - FIRST CALCULATE PI/18
      PIE18=4.0*ATAN(1.0)/18.0
C INITIATE THE LOOP COUNTER
      ITHETA=0
   10 THETA=FLOAT(ITHETA)*PIE18
      S=SIN(THETA)
      WRITE(6,20)THETA,S
   20 FORMAT(9H SINE OF ,F10.5,12H RADIANS IS ,F10.5)
C INCREMENT THE LOOP COUNTER
      ITHETA=ITHETA+1
C TEST FOR COMPLETION OF THE LOOP COUNT
      IF(ITHETA.LE.9)GO TO 10
      STOP
      END
```

SUMMARY: To form a counting loop:
           Before the loop initialize an integer counter.
           At the end of the loop increment and test the counter.
           Remove invariant calculations from the loop.
           If a series of real values is required, derive them from
           the integer counter.

PROBLEM 3.5.   Write a program to find the factorial of a positive
   integer.

N! = N(N-1)(N-2) .... (2)(1)
0! is defined to be 1

PROBLEM 3.6. Often an analytic expression for the integrand of a function cannot be found, and a numerical form of integration must be used. The procedures are called "numerical quadrature" because the term "numerical integration" is more usually applied to a different situation (see Problem 3.7). About the simplest method is the trapezoidal rule, which finds the area under a segment of curve as in Fig. 3.10, in which

$$\int_{x_1}^{x_2} f(x)\,dx = \frac{f(x_1)+f(x_2)}{2}\,(x_2-x_1)$$

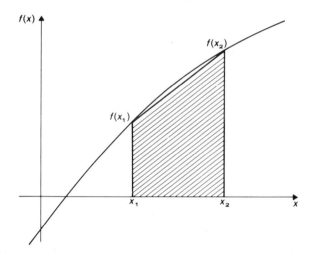

Fig.3.10. Illustrating the trapezoidal rule.

Usually a single trapezoid would not provide an accurate result, so that a number of thin trapezoids are normally taken and their areas summed. This leads to a simplification of the formula

$$\int_{x_0}^{x_n} f(x)\,dx = h\left\{\frac{f(x_0)}{2} + f(x_1) + \ldots\ldots + f(x_{n-1}) + \frac{f(x_n)}{2}\right\}$$

for n trapezoids of equal width h between x_0 and x_n, for which

$$h = x_1 - x_0 = x_2 - x_1 = \ldots = x_n - x_{n-1}$$

Using the trapezoidal rule, find

$$\int_0^1 f(x)\,dx = 0.5 + \frac{1}{\sqrt{2\pi}} \int_0^1 e^{-x^2/2}\,dx$$

by dividing the range $0 \leqslant x \leqslant 1$ into n equal segments. Write the program so that different values of n can be tried. What value of n gives the result which is accurate to 0.1%?

(The correct answer is .8413, found within .1% when n = 5)

PROBLEM 3.7:   The usual meaning of "numerical integration" is in the solution of differential equations. Suppose the equation

$$\frac{dy}{dt} = f(y,t)$$

is to be solved with an "initial condition" given as

$$y(t_0) = y_0$$

Euler's method of numerical integration uses one term only from the expansion

$$y(t+h) = y(t) + hy'(t) + h^2 \frac{y''(t)}{2} + \ldots$$

to predict $y(t+h)$ by the formula

$$y(t+h) = y(t) + hy'(t)$$

$$= y(t) + hf(y,t)$$

The procedure is to predict $y(t_0+h)$ from y_0, then from it $y(t_0+2h)$ and so on. Not surprisingly, the method is neither accurate nor stable in most cases. However, it does serve to illustrate the concept of numerical integration.

(i)   Write a program to solve numerically

$$\frac{dy}{dt} = \cos y$$

from $t = 0$ to $t = 2\pi$, given that $y(0) = 0.5$. How many steps must be used to give an accuracy of 0.1% in $y(2\pi)$?

(ii)   Also solve

$$\frac{dy}{dt} = \frac{1}{\sqrt{2\pi}} e^{-t^2/2}$$

by Euler's method from $t = 0$ to $t = 1$, given that $y(0) = 0.5$. How small must h be to give an accuracy of 0.1% in $y(1)$ and how does this approach compare to the trapezoidal rule as a method of numerical quadrature?

9 Automatic Loop Control – the DO and CONTINUE statements

Having seen in the previous section how to arrange a repeated
calculation it is not surprising that FORTRAN includes an automatic
facility for organising loops which initializes, increments, and
tests the loop variable. With this facility repeated sections of
the program are begun with the DO statement and may end on almost
any statement;   however the usual practice is to end them on a
CONTINUE statement.

EXAMPLE: In the previous section the printing of a table of sines
   was used as an illustration of loop control using an IF statement.
   Using DO and CONTINUE statements, this same example now becomes

```
C PRINT A TABLE OF SINES - FIRST CALCULATE PI/18
        PIE18=4.Ø*ATAN(1.Ø)/18.Ø
        DO 3Ø ITHETA=1,1Ø
        THETA=FLOAT(ITHETA-1)*PIE18
        S=SIN(THETA)
        WRITE(6,2Ø)THETA,S
    2Ø FORMAT(9H SINE OF ,F1Ø.5,12H RADIANS IS ,F1Ø.5)
    3Ø CONTINUE
        STOP
        END
```

Here the statements between the DO and CONTINUE statements are to be
repeated with ITHETA taking the successive values 1, 2, 3, ..., 10.
The angle THETA is a real variable and is derived from ITHETA.   Note
that the arithmetic statement that does this is different now.   This
is because one of the rules about DO loops will not allow ITHETA to
start from zero.   Again for efficiency the value of PIE18 is
calculated before the loop begins rather than each time it is
repeated.

The general form of the DO - statement is

     DO *sn iv* = *ivc1, ivc2, ivc3*

where *sn* means statement number
      iv means integer variable
     ivc means integer variable or constant

The statements following the DO statement up to and including the
one with statement number *sn* are repeated with the integer variable
iv taking the values *ivc1, ivc1+ivc3, ivc1+2*ivc3*, ... until *ivc2*

is exceeded, whence the DO is said to be "satisfied". However,
regardless of the relationship of *iv* to *ivc2*, the loop is always
done *at least once*. This rule is a source of much program error
(and is different from some other languages including BASIC). *Ivc3*
is optional and if it is not given then 1 is used as the increment.

EXAMPLES:

 (i)   DO 15 K = 1,12,2   This loop is repeated 6 times
              :   with K = 1,3,5,7,9,11
              :
       15 CONTINUE

 (ii)   DO 3∅ ITHETA = 1,1∅   This loop is repeated 10 times
              :   with ITHETA = 1,2,3,4,5,6,7,8,9,10
              :
       3∅ CONTINUE

 (iii)   IQ = 5
           DO 999 IZ = 6,IQ   This loop is executed once with
              :   IZ = 6
              :
       999 CONTINUE

The detailed rules affecting DO loops are:

sn - statement number. Somewhere following the DO statement there
     must be a statement with number *sn*. This must be an executable
     statement other than STOP, RETURN (Chapter 4), or an arithmetic
     IF. A logical IF can be used, but what occurs will depend on the
     logical expression. If .TRUE. the statement of the IF is
     obeyed which could or could not cause transfer away from the
     loop. If .FALSE. then looping continues normally. The
     statements from the DO up to and including *sn* are called the
     "range" of the DO. The range is always executed at least once.
     Control may not be transfered into the range from outside - a
     loop must always be entered with the DO statement.

iv - integer variable. This is called the "index" of the DO; only
     integer varaibles are allowed. It may not be modified within
     the range. It takes on the successive values *ivc1*, *ivc1* + *ivc3*,
     ivc1 + 2*ivc3*, ... as the loop is repeated until it exceeds
     ivc2. However, regardless of the relationship of the index to
     ivc2, the range is always executed the first time, when
     iv = *ivc1*. If a control statement causes a jump out of the
     range of a DO, the index is available with its last value for
     further computation. But if the DO is satisfied normally, the

index is *not* available for further computation. This is an awkward rule which is the root of many program errors and is best illustrated by examples:

(i)   Control transferred out of the DO

```
      DO 3Ø INDEX = 1,1Ø
         :
      IF(INDEX.EQ.5)GO TO 5Ø
         :
  3Ø  CONTINUE
         :
  5Ø  WRITE(6,6Ø)INDEX           The value printed will be 5
  6Ø  FORMAT(1X,I5)
         :
```

(ii)   The DO is satisfied normally

```
      DO 3Ø  INDEX = 1,1Ø
         :
  3Ø  CONTINUE
      WRITE(6,6Ø)INDEX            This is dangerous.  The value
  6Ø  FORMAT(1X,I5)              printed may be 11 or rubbish.
         :
```

(iii)   Clever programmers have a way around this

```
      DO 3Ø INDEX = 1,1Ø
      I=INDEX
         :
  3Ø  CONTINUE
      WRITE(6,6Ø)I                The value printed will be 10
  6Ø  FORMAT(1X,I5)
```

ivc1,ivc2,ivc3 - integer variables or constants. If constants they must be greater than zero. If variables they must be unsubscripted (Chapter 5). The initial value of the index is *ivc1*. The test value for loop completion is *ivc2*. The increment is *ivc3*, or if it is not given, 1. None of these may be adjusted during the loop.

These rules may seem complicated, but straightforward programming will not usually run foul of them. It is only when trying something a bit fancy that a programmer is likely to get caught. The most likely sources of trouble are:

  (i)   That loops are always done at least once.
 (ii)   That the index is not available after normal completion.
(iii)   That the range may not be entered from the outside.
 (iv)   That the index and other loop parameters may not be adjusted
       within the range.

   DO loops may be nested in standard FORTRAN IV to any depth, but on
some computers there are restrictions (one widely available medium-
sized computer allows only 3). A nest is a group of loops contained
one within the other, i.e. the range of an inner loop is entirely
within the range of the outer. Nested loops must use different
integer variables as index and they are not allowed to cross; legal
and illegal situations are illustrated below.

       Permitted   *Not Permitted*

The loops are nested   The loops are crossed

```
        DO 20 I = 1,10                  DO 30 I = 1,10
          .                               .
          .                               .
        DO 20 J = 1,10                  DO 20 J = 1,10
          .                               .
          .                               .
        DO 10 K = 1,5                   DO 30 K = 1,5
          .                               .
          .                               .
     10 CONTINUE                     20 CONTINUE
          .                               .
          .                               .
     20 CONTINUE                     30 CONTINUE
```

   The CONTINUE statement which has appeared in the above examples is
not, strictly speaking, absolutely necessary; it is actually a
"dummy" statement which performs no computation. However, when
provided with a statement number it allows the programmer to join up
bits of his program. It is generally considered to be good form to
terminate a DO loop on a CONTINUE statement, and they can be very
useful as destinations for GO TO statements and IF statements.
(Conversely a programmer who ends a DO loop on an IF statement is
displaying poor form.)

EXAMPLE: Suppose it is desired to evaluate 10 terms of the Fibonacci
   series which is defined by the recurrence:

$$x_n = x_{n-1} + x_{n-2}$$

A DO loop is used to count the terms, and the recurrence is

FEATURE : AUTOMATIC LOOP CONTROL

FORTRAN	BASIC

```
DO sn=ivc1,ivc2,ivc3          line no. FOR variable = expr 1 TO expr 2 STEP expr 3
     .                             .
     .                             .
     sn executable statement   line number NEXT variable
```

The program between the DO statement and the statement numbered sn is called the range of the DO and is executed with the index iv having values $ivc1$, $ivc1+ivc3$, $ivc1+2*ivc3$,.... until $ivc2$ is exceeded, when the DO is satisfied. The range is always executed at least once.

The program between these two statements is executed with variable having values expression 1, expression 1 + expression 3, expression 1 + 2* expression 3, ... until expression 2 is exceeded.
The loop will be jumped over if expression 1, expression 2, and expression 3 are such that it should not be executed.

Rules:

iv can only be an integer variable. It may not be adjusted in the range. If control is transferred out of the range before the DO is satisfied, then the index iv is available for use in further computation. If the DO is satisfied normally then the value of the index is not available for further computation.

Rules:

variable can be any variable. It can be adjusted anywhere in the program. Its value is available anywhere in the program.

$ivc1$, $ivc2$, $ivc3$ are integer variables or positive integer constants greater than zero. If variables they may not be subscripted. If $ivc3$ is omitted it is taken as 1. None of these parameters may be adjusted within the range of the loop.

The expressions may not be adjusted while looping.

If STEP expression 3 is omitted it is taken as 1.

executable statement may not be STOP, RETURN, or an arithmetic IF. It is usual to use the CONTINUE statement.

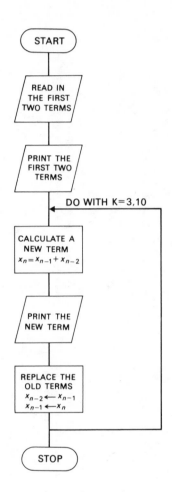

Fig.3.11. Evaluation of the Fibonacci series by recurrence. **Note** the replacement of x_{n-2} and x_{n-1}.

expedited by self-replacement of variables X2 and X1. The program could be

```
C A PROGRAM TO EVALUATE THE FIBONACCI  SERIES
C READ IN AND PRINT THE FIRST TWO TERMS
      WRITE(6,1Ø)
  1Ø FORMAT(17H FIBONACCI SERIES,/,2ØH THE FIRST TWO TERMS)
      READ(5,2Ø)X1,X2
  2Ø FORMAT(2F1Ø.5)
      WRITE(6,3Ø)X1,X2
  3Ø FORMAT(1X,2F1Ø.5)
C USE A DO LOOP TO OBTAIN 8 MORE TERMS
      DO 5Ø K = 3,1Ø
      X=X1+X2
      WRITE(6,4Ø)K,X
  4Ø FORMAT(6H TERM ,I3,3H IS,F1Ø.5)
C REPLACE X1 and X2 FOR THE NEXT RECURRENCE
      X2=X1
      X1=X
  5Ø CONTINUE
      STOP
      END
```

A flow diagram is shown in Fig. 3.11.

10 An Aside—more about FORMAT—slashes and commas

The Fibonacci series example has a new feature in its FORMAT statement, the / (slash) which makes output (or input) move to a new line (or card). Every READ or WRITE statement begins a new line (or card) as a matter of course. However it is often desirable to start a new line (or card) in the middle of a READ or WRITE *list*. A / (slash) encountered in a FORMAT accomplishes this.

The statements

```
      WRITE(6,33)X,Y,P,Q,R,S
  33 FORMAT(12H RESULTS ARE,3(2F8.3,2X))
```

would produce the message and all six results on one line. By writing

```
      WRITE(6,33)X,Y,P,Q,R,S
  33 FORMAT(12H RESULTS ARE /3(2X,2F8.3))
```

```
                    FEATURE : DUMMY STATEMENT

        FORTRAN                          BASIC

        CONTINUE                 No such facility

The statement does not result in
any action.  It usually will
have a statement number and is
used to join together programs
particularly as the last statement
in the range of a DO loop.
```

```
                FEATURE : NEW LINES IN PRINTING

        FORTRAN                          BASIC

The / specification in a FORMAT     No such facility on input or
statement starts a new line for     output except in the use of
output or a new line (or card)      separate PRINT statements.
for input.
```

the message comes on one line with the six results on the next line;
note the moving of the 2X to keep the first space clear. Finally,

```
      WRITE(6,33)X,Y,P,Q,R,S,
 33 FORMAT(12H RESULTS ARE /(2X,2F8.3))
```

puts the message on one line and two results on each of the next
three lines.

The vigilant will have noted that commas were not used to
separate out the slashes. The truth can now be told about the comma;
it can be left out wherever there is no ambiguity as a result.

Therefore

```
 5Ø FORMAT(1X,F1Ø.8)
```

could be

```
 5Ø FORMAT(1XF1Ø.8)
```

```
 4Ø FORMAT(5H TERM,I3,3H IS,F1Ø.5)
```

could be

```
 4Ø FORMAT(5H TERM I3,3H IS F1Ø.8)
```

In general the comma can be left out:

  (i)   before or after /
 (ii)   after X
(iii)   after a message.

It is only absolutely necessary where it separates numbers
associated with adjacent fields. However, since good programming
is clear programming, it is not always such a good thing to leave it
out.

PROBLEM 3.8: Write programs using DO loops to find:

(a) The factorial of a number
(b) The number of permutations of n items taken r at a time,

$$ {}_nP_r = \frac{n!}{r!} $$

(c) The number of combinations of n items taken r at a time,

$$_n C_r = \frac{n!}{r!\,(n-r)!}$$

PROBLEM 3.9: Write a program to evaluate up to 10 terms of the power series for sin x

$$\sin x = x - \frac{x^3}{3!} + \frac{x^5}{5!} - \frac{x^7}{7!} + \ldots\ldots\ldots$$

For efficiency work out a recurrence relationship for the terms of the series. Use a DO loop to count to 10 terms but exit from the calculation if you know that the *next* term will contribute less than .01% of the series. Print the result and the number of terms used.

PROBLEM 3.10: Write a program to find and print all the prime factors of an integer. To do this, simply test for a zero remainder using the MOD function, with every divisor less than the number. If a zero remainder is found, it remains to test if that divisor is itself prime, by trying every number between zero and its square root. If you draw a flow diagram this is not a difficult problem; there are ways of making it more efficient.

11 Other Forms of Control—the arithmetic IF, assigned and computed GO TO

The quaint arithmetic IF statement was the only IF statement in early versions of FORTRAN. It considers the result of an arithmetic expression and takes one of three branches depending on whether the expression is negative, zero or positive. This is not, of course, quite the way that programmers think about decisions and so in practice the logical IF is nearly always used. The form of the arithmetic IF is:

IF(*expression*)*sn1,sn2,sn3*

> *expression* is an arithmetic expression which, as usual should be real or integer but not a mixture.
>
> *sn1, sn2, sn3* are three statement numbers. Program control is transferred to one of these three as follows:
>
> > *sn1* if *expression* is negative
> >
> > *sn2* if *expression* is zero
> >
> > *sn3* if *expression* is positive

The order then is easy to remember as minus, zero, plus. If *expression* is real the result is likely to be zero only by accident. The statement immediately following the IF is usually one of those

numbered *sn1, sn2, sn3*;   if it has no statement number it cannot be
reached at all.

EXAMPLE:

$$IF(B*B-4.*A*C)2\emptyset,3\emptyset,4\emptyset$$

which is quite obviously the test for a zero discriminant in a
quadratic expression ax^2 + bx + x.   This is one of the few obvious
situations where the arithmetic IF would be used.

The computed GO TO statement enables a large number of destinations
to be given which depend on the value of a nonsubscripted integer
variable.   It is written

GO TO(*sn1,sn2,.......*),*iv*

This relatively useless statement will jump to *sn1* if *iv* is 1, *sn2*
if *iv* is 2, etc.   *iv* must have a value between 1 and the number of
specified destinations.   Again the next statement in the program
will be unreachable unless it has a statement number which would
usually but not necessarily be one of those in the list.

EXAMPLE

GO TO ($1\emptyset,2\emptyset,4\emptyset,3\emptyset$),INDEX

INDEX must be 1, 2, 3 or 4.   The transfer takes place to

statement 10 if INDEX is 1
statement 20 if INDEX is 2
statement 40 if INDEX is 3
statement 30 if INDEX is 4

Finally, FORTRAN has the ASSIGN statement and the assigned GO TO
statement which allow the programmer to change the destination of a
GO TO elsewhere in his program.   This can be very useful.

The assigned GO TO is

GO TO *iv*(*sn1,sn2, ...*)

iv is a nonsubscripted integer variable whose value is the
destination statement number, but this value must be established in
an ASSIGN statement.   The list *sn1, sn2,* ... must contain all the
possible statement numbers that can be assigned.

```
┌─────────────────────────────────────────────────────────────────┐
│              FEATURE : ARITHMETIC IF STATEMENT                  │
│                                                                 │
│              IF  (expression) sn1, sn2, sn3                     │
│                                                                 │
│  Expression is an arithmetic expression in either real or integer│
│  mode                                                           │
│                                                                 │
│  If expression is negative execution jumps to statement number sn1│
│                                                                 │
│  If expression is zero     execution jumps to statement number sn2│
│                                                                 │
│  If expression is positive execution jumps to statement number sn3│
└─────────────────────────────────────────────────────────────────┘
```

```
┌─────────────────────────────────────────────────────────────────┐
│              FEATURE : COMPUTED GO TO STATEMENT                 │
│                                                                 │
│              GO TO (sn1, sn2, sn3 .....), iv                    │
│                                                                 │
│  iv is a nonsubscripted integer variable which must have a value│
│  between 1 and the number of statement numbers given.          │
│                                                                 │
│  If iv = 1 execution jumps to statement number sn1             │
│  If iv = 2 execution jumps to statement number sn2             │
│  If iv = 3 execution jumps to statement number sn3             │
│                           etc.                                  │
└─────────────────────────────────────────────────────────────────┘
```

```
┌─────────────────────────────────────────────────────────────────┐
│              FEATURE : ASSIGNED GO TO STATEMENT                 │
│                                                                 │
│              GO TO iv (sn1, sn2, sn3 ....)                      │
│                                                                 │
│  Execution jumps to statement number iv                        │
│                                                                 │
│  iv is a nonsubscripted integer variable assigned a value in a │
│  previous ASSIGN statement which is one of those statement numbers│
│  given.                                                         │
│                                                                 │
│  sn1, sn2, sn3 ... are the possible statement numbers which may be│
│  assigned to iv.                                                │
│                                                                 │
│              ASSIGN sn TO iv                                    │
│                                                                 │
│  Statement number sn is assigned to nonsubscripted integer     │
│  variables iv for use in a later assigned GO TO statement.     │
│                                                                 │
│  sn must occur in the list of statement numbers in the assigned GO TO.│
└─────────────────────────────────────────────────────────────────┘
```

The ASSIGN statement

> ASSIGN *sn* TO *iv*

assigns the statement number *sn* to the integer variable *iv* for use in an assigned GO TO statement. *sn* must be one of those listed in the assigned GO TO.

EXAMPLE:

> ASSIGN 34 TO JOHN
> :
> :
> GO TO JOHN(1Ø,2Ø,16,34,99)

This combination results in a transfer to statement number 34.

12 Supplementary Problems

PROBLEM 3.11   Write a program to find the Least Common Multiple (LCM) of two integers. As an example, the LCM of 6 and 4 is 12.

PROBLEM 3.12   Write a program to find the Greatest Common Factor (GCF) of two integers. As an example, the GCF of 105 and 84 is 7.

PROBLEM 3.13   Write a program to find all the common prime factors of two integers. As an example, the common prime factors of 105 and 84 are 7 and 3.

PROBLEM 3.14   In problem 3.9, a power series was used to evaluate sin x. Many useful functions can be evaluated using power series, including

$$e^x = 1 + x + \frac{x^2}{2!} + \frac{x^3}{3!} + \ldots$$

$$\ln(1+x) = x - \frac{x^2}{2} + \frac{x^3}{3} - \frac{x^4}{4}$$

$$\sin x = x - \frac{x^3}{3!} + \frac{x^5}{5!} - \frac{x^7}{7!} + \ldots$$

$$\cos x = 1 - \frac{x^2}{2!} + \frac{x^4}{4!} - \frac{x^6}{6!} + \ldots$$

Derive recurrence relationships for all these series. Do these relationships give any guidance in estimating the residual errors and the expected rates of convergence for these series? Program each series and verify these expectations.

PROBLEM 3.15   Many games can be devised to be played with the
computer. With complex games, such as chess, no optimum strategy
is known and programming these is a very deep study. However for
many simple games optimum strategies are possible. Such a game is
NIMB, which can always be won by the first player. Write a program
to play the simplified version described below. A good program
will issue instructions and information as the game proceeds;
furthermore it will never lose if given the first move or if the
opponent makes a mistake.

The game in a simplified version begins with the number 15, which
could represent for example 15 matches on a table. Each of the
two players in turn must remove one, two, or three from the number
available. The loser is the player forced to remove the last one.
The winning strategy is very simple.

PROBLEM 3.16   If NIMB was mastered without much difficulty, try
noughts and crosses (X's and 0's). Here, either player can force
a draw. If a player makes a mistake, the other can win.

4 Functions and Subroutines

1 Introduction

FORTRAN has endured for many years as the principal computing
language for scientific and technical calculation, and one reason
for this is found in the superior facilities for defining and using
functions and subroutines. The features described in the previous
chapters are the foundations of the language but they are not
particularly unusual (or convenient) by comparison with other languages. It is with functions and subroutines that a programmer can
begin to generalize his algorithms to form independent program
modules which can be used wherever convenient, and communicated
through program libraries to be of use to other people. Subroutines
for many thousands of applications are available so that the FORTRAN
programmer can benefit from the work of others.

This relatively short chapter is of great importance in learning
to use FORTRAN effectively. The problems not only illustrate the
new facilities but also review the fundamentals already covered.
The student should use this chapter to consolidate his grasp of
FORTRAN before proceeding.

2 Arithmetic Statement Functions

The simplest kind of defined function is the arithmetic statement
function, which can be included in any FORTRAN program in a single
defining statement. It can be used within that program as a function
just as if it were a built-in function. The function is given a
name and a list of arguments. Many versions of FORTRAN require that
the function definition be at the beginning of the program and so it
is safest to have all the arithmetic statement functions together
just before the first executable statement of a program.

EXAMPLE: The statement

$$DISC(A,B,C)=B*B-4.\emptyset*A*C$$

defines a function called DISC, which is a real function* because

---

* As will be seen in the next Chapter, it can be forced to be an integer function.

of the spelling of its name, with three real arguments A, B, and
C. This function evidently evaluates the discriminant of a
quadratic expression $ax^2 + bx + c$. Therefore the statement

$$IF(DISC(1.,1.,1.))1\emptyset,2\emptyset,3\emptyset$$

uses the DISC function to test the discriminant of

$$x^2 + x + 1 = 0$$

which is negative. In this case the branch would be taken to
statement number 10. The arguments of the function are called
dummy arguments because in using the function other arguments are
substituted for them. Therefore the function DISC does not
actually use variables A, B, or C even if they occur in the program.
Instead it uses the values of whatever arguments it is given when
invoked. The arguments can be expressions themselves involving
other functions.

If a function definition should happen to have variables on the
right hand side which do not appear as arguments, then these are
considered to be variables which will be defined elsewhere in the
program and their actual values are used when the function is invoked
as the examples will show. A function must have at least one
argument.

Arithmetic statement function definitions, then, appear together
at the beginning of a program and take the form

name (arguments) = arithmetic expression

The type of function (real or integer) is implied by *name*. The
type of each argument is implied by its form, and the *arithmetic
expression* will also have its own type. When the function is used,
the *arithmetic expression* is evaluated using the values of the
arguments given. The result will be converted if necessary to be
the same type as the function. Therefore there are many combinations
of type possible in the function, its *arguments*, and the *arithmetic
expression*. The function *name* can be invoked anywhere in the same
program.*

---

* By this is meant anywhere from the beginning of the program, which is where
the functions should be defined, to the END statement. As will be seen, a
subroutine is a separate program according to this definition.

FEATURE : ARITHMETIC STATEMENT FUNCTIONS

FORTRAN	BASIC
name (dummy variables) = expression	*line number* DEF FN*a* (*dummy variable*) = *expression*
name is the name of the function and implicitly defines the type of the result (real or integer).	FN*a* is the name of the function - *a* can be any letter from A to Z. For example FNQ.
dummy variables in a list of variable names separated by commas which *expression* refers to for the arguments of the function; there must be at least one.	*dummy variable* is a variable name which *expression* refers to for the arguments of the function. Usually there can only be one.
When the function *name (arguments)* is referred to in an arithemtic expression any variables, constants or expressions of the correct type are substituted as *arguments* in one-to-one correspondence with the *dummy variables*. The result comes from using the values of the *arguments* in place of the *dummy variables* in the evaluation of the defining *expression*.	When the function FN*a* (argument) is referred to in an expression, any quantity is used as *argument* and the result comes from a substitution of the value of *argument* for the *dummy variable* in *expression*.
Other variable names may be used in *expression* which are not given as *dummy variables* in which case they should be variables defined in the program before the function is used. Their actual values are then used to evaluate *expression*.	Other variable names than *dummy variable* may be used in *expression*, in which case they should be variables defined in the program before the function is invoked. Their actual values are then used to evaluate *expression*.
A function *name* must not be defined more than once and it is best that it should occur at the beginning of the program.	A function FN*a* should be defined only once, but it may be anywhere in the program before its first use.

EXAMPLE: The statement

ROUND(X)=AINT(X+Ø.5)

defines a real arithmetic statement function of one real argument
for rounding of positive numbers. When it is used, the real
argument is rounded to the next highest whole number. The result
is still of type real. In the program which follows this definition,
the following statements might occur:

Y=ROUND(1.3)   produces the result Y = 1.0
X=ROUND(4.7)   produces the result X = 5.0. Do not confuse
               the X of the definition which is a "dummy"
               with the real variable X.
Z=4.Ø*ATAN(1.Ø)
X=ROUND(Z)   produces the result X = 3.0

EXAMPLE: The conversion function

CONVER(IDUM)=FLOAT(IDUM)*CONST

is a real function which multiplies its integer argument by the
real conversion factor CONST. Because CONST is not an argument
of the function, it is a real variable of the program. IDUM is a
dummy integer variable. The statement

CONST=Ø.4536

or

DATA CONST/Ø.4536/   (see Chapter 5)

would define the conversion from pounds to kilograms and following
this statement

XKGS=CONVER(5)

would produce the kilogram equivalent of 5 pounds, 2.268 Kg. The
same function with different values of CONST could provide other
conversions.

EXAMPLE: Two real functions of two real arguments

XCORD (R,THETA)=R*COS(THETA)
YCORD (R,THETA)=R*SIN(THETA)

provide the conversion of polar co-ordinates (R,THETA) to Cartesian
form.

Similarly

$$RADIUS(X,Y)=SQRT(X*X+Y*Y)$$
$$ANGLE(X,Y)=ATAN2(Y,X)$$

defines the inverse relationship.

PROBLEM 4.1: Write and test arithmetic statement functions for

(i)   Hyperbolic sine and cosine

$$\sinh x = \frac{e^x - e^{-x}}{2} \qquad \cosh x = \frac{e^x + e^{-x}}{2}$$

(ii)   The "sign" of an integer number, giving the integer result

-1 if the number is negative
+1 if the number is zero or positive

(iii)   The real area of a triangle from the given integer coordinates of its vertices, Fig. 4.1

$$area = \tfrac{1}{2} \left| y_2(x_3 - x_1) + y_1(x_2 - x_3) + y_3(x_1 - x_2) \right|$$

(iv)   The given order of coordinates in (iii) will be either
clockwise or anticlockwise, and without taking the absolute value
the area formula gives a positive result for clockwise coordinates
and a negative result for anticlockwise ones.   Return the integer
result

+1 for clockwise coordinates
 0 if indeterminant (zero area)
-1 for anticlockwise coordinates

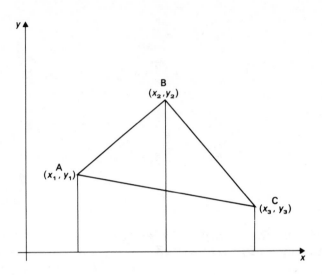

Fig.4.1. The area of a triangle can be calculated from the co-ordinates
of its vertices.

PROBLEM 4.2:   In problem 3.6 the area under a curve was found by the
trapezoidal rule.   Rewrite this program to use an arithmetic
statement function to provide f(x).   Find to 0.1% accuracy

(i) $0.5 + \dfrac{1}{\sqrt{2\pi}} \displaystyle\int_0^1 e^{-x^2/2} \, dx$

(ii) $\displaystyle\int_0^{\pi/2} \dfrac{dx}{\sqrt{1 - \dfrac{\sin^2 x}{4}}}$

The program will be more general if you read in the upper limit of
integration and the number of segments to divide the integral into.

PROBLEM 4.3:   In problem 3.3 the convergence of the method of False
Position was accelerated using Aitken's delta-squared process.
Rewrite this program to use arithmetic statement functions to
replace calculations which are common to different parts of the
program.   Solve:

(i) $x + \sin x = 0.5$

(ii) $e^x = 2x^2$

3 Function Subprograms—the FUNCTION and RETURN statements

A single statement defining a function has its obvious limitations;
many useful functions could be established if more than the single
line allowed by the arithmetic statement function could be used.
Because of this a facility exists for creating multiple line functions
to incorporate any combination of FORTRAN statements. This allows
the programmer to write his function as a separate "subprogram",
being a distinct deck or "module" beginning with a FUNCTION statement and ending with its own END statement. Such functions introduce
a concept very important in FORTRAN - that of local variables. These
allow the subprogram to use any variable names and still be isolated
from the "main program". This makes FORTRAN subprograms theoretically
portable in the sense that they should be able to work in *any* FORTRAN
program without worry about interference between the variables "local"
to the subprogram and those belonging to other parts of the program.

The FUNCTION statement defines the name of the function and its
arguments:

FUNCTION *name* (*dummy variables*)

The type of function (real or integer) is implicitly established by
name according to the usual rules. So too are the types of the
various function arguments listed as a series of *dummy variable*
names separated by commas.

The FUNCTION statement is followed by a program of any complexity
which works out the value of the function. At least once in this
program the value must be assigned by a statement assigning it to
name

name = *expression*

and the completion of the function is signalled by the RETURN statement of which there could be several in a complicated function:

RETURN

Because the function is a separate program, it must have the END
statement as its last statement

END

As an example, a function to evaluate the integer factorial of an

integer number is listed below. This function will return the value
zero and print a rude message if its single argument is negative.
The factorial of the integer argument is returned otherwise,
including the value 1 for the factorial of 0. Fig. 4.2 is a flow
diagram of the subprogram.

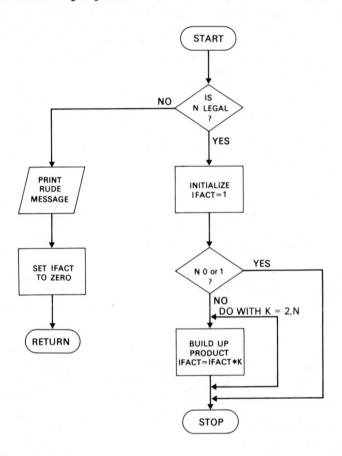

Fig.4.2. Flow diagram of a FUNCTION subprogram
to evaluate the factorial of N.

Note that because DO-loops are always executed once, an IF statement
has been used to jump around the loop if it is not wanted.

```
      FUNCTION IFACT(N)
C A FUNCTION TO EVALUATE THE FACTORIAL OF N
C CHECK THAT N IS LEGAL
      IF(N.LT.Ø)GO TO 97
      IFACT=1
C EXIT IF NO LOOP REQUIRED
      IF(N.LE.1) GO TO 2Ø
C ACCUMULATE PRODUCT IN LOOP
      DO 1Ø K=2,N
      IFACT=IFACT*K
   1Ø CONTINUE
   2Ø RETURN
C N WAS ILLEGAL ... PRINT MESSAGE AND RETURN ZERO
   97 WRITE(6,98) N
   98 FORMAT(11H FACTORIAL ,I1Ø,16H CANNOT BE FOUND)
      IFACT=Ø
      RETURN
      END
```

This program has two RETURN statements, and one END. Their meaning
should not be confused. The END statement does nothing in the
execution of a program, it simply indicates the physical end of
FORTRAN programs or subprograms. The RETURN statement is active in
the execution of a program since it signals that the evaluation of
the function is complete. Therefore RETURN is an executable statement whereas END is not.

How then is this function used? The FUNCTION subprogram and the
"main program" which uses it are presented to the computer together.
The main program usually comes first with its own END statement as
the last one, followed by the FUNCTION statement, and the rest of the
function up to and including its END statement. Other functions
could then follow, as could other kinds of subprogram including
SUBROUTINES which are introduced later in this chapter. Fig. 4.3
illustrates the usual structure of a FORTRAN program with subprograms.
In a batch situation some computers require separate "control cards"
between the modules; it is beyond the scope of this course to
describe them all.

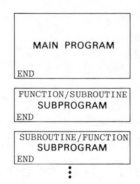

(a) As a listing on a timesharing system.

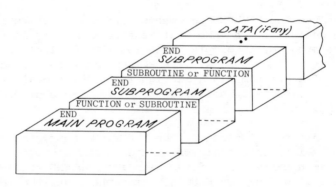

(b) As a card deck for batch work.

Fig.4.3. The layout of a FORTRAN program with subprograms.

A suitable main program using the function IFACT to evaluate and print all the factorials from 1 to 10 is then:

```
C A MAIN PROGRAM TO PRINT FACTORIALS FROM 1 TO 1Ø
      DO 2Ø K=1,1Ø
C OBTAIN FACTORIAL FROM THE FUNCTION IFACT
      IJ=IFACT(K)
      WRITE(6,1Ø)K,IJ
   1Ø FORMAT(11H FACTORIAL ,I1Ø,4H IS , I1Ø)
   2Ø CONTINUE
      STOP
      END
```

In both the FUNCTION and the main program a variable K has been used. Because these are separate programs they are not the same; they are "local" variables which means that they are completely unrelated. In practice this means that a FUNCTION subprogram does not interfere with any variables of the main program because they are not shared. The exception to this is that the arguments of the function are shared. Thus if these programs are used together, the values 1, 2, ..., 10 taken by K are used in the factorial subroutine as variable N.

Therefore it follows - and this is very important - that if N were adjusted or changed in the subprogram, then this change would be carried back as a change in the main program variable K. It is unusual and altogether too fancy to do this deliberately in a FUNCTION subprogram, although as will be seen it is quite usual in subroutines. In this example it could be quite catastrophic since the main program variable K is the index of a DO loop.

It is possible to get into serious and elusive trouble if a subprogram by adjusting one of its arguments turns out to have adjusted a constant rather than a variable! The main program is, in effect, wrecked.

PROBLEM 4.4: Try the factorial function by writing a different main program which reads in a number whose factorial is evaluated and printed. The factorials of even modest integers are very large. How large a factorial can your computer manage? Be careful with the output format.

PROBLEM 4.5: Write the functions to find:

(i) $_nC_r = \dfrac{n!}{r!\,(n-r)!}$ Is the result always integer?

(ii) $_nP_r = \dfrac{n!}{(n-r)!}$ Is the result always integer?

A FUNCTION subprogram can include arithmetic statement functions which, like variables in the subprograms, are local to the FUNCTION only. As before they should precede the first executable statement of the FUNCTION; the FUNCTION statement itself is not executable and the arithmetic statement function definitions should be between the FUNCTION statement and the first executable statement.

```
                        FEATURE : FUNCTION SUBPROGRAMS
                FORTRAN                              BASIC
```

The structure is

FUNCTION *name* (*dummy variables*)

     :

name = *expression*

     :

RETURN

     :

END

The structure is

line number DEF FN*a* (*dummy variables*)

     :

line number LET FN*a* = *expression*

     :

line number   FNEND

name is the name of the function and implicitly defines the type of the result (real or integer).

FN*a* is the name of the function. *a* can be any letter from A to Z.

dummy variables is a list of variable names separated by commas which are used in the function as *arguments*. Any variable name used in the function and not included in the *dummy variable* list is local to the function.

dummy variables is a list of variable names separated by commas which are used in the function as its *arguments*. Any variable name used in the function and not included in the *dummy variable* list is local to the function.

When the function *name* (*arguments*) is referred to using variables, constants or expressions of the correct type, their values are passed to the subprogram where they are used as the values of the *dummy variables*. The subprogram can modify its *arguments* but care must then be taken never to use it so that constants are affected.

When the function FN*a* (*arguments*) is referred to, the values of the *arguments* are passed to the function where they are used as the values of the *dummy variables*. The function can modify its *arguments* but care must be taken never to use it so that constants are affected.

Within the subprogram a statement must assign a value to *name* which is then passed back as the function value.

Within the subprogram a value must be assigned to FN*a* in a LET statement which is then passed back as the function value.

The RETURN statement indicates when the evaluation is finished; there can be several.

The FNEND statement indicates when the evaluation is finished; there can be only one.

The END statement must be the last one of the subprogram.

The FNEND statement must be the last one of the function.

PROBLEM 4.6: Here's a challenge! Incorporating an arithmetic
statement function which gives the sign of a triangle according
to the order of its vertices (Problem 4.1 (v)), write a function
to find out if a *fourth* pair of integer Cartesian co-ordinates is
inside or outside that triangle. Return the integer value 0 for
outside and 1 for inside.

4 Another FORMAT Specification—the E field

The exponential form of real constants was encountered in Chapter 2.
Using it very large or very small numbers could be written with a
multiplying exponential, i.e.

3.ØE1Ø	meant	3×10^{10}
16.35E-4	meant	0.001635

Sometimes very large or small real numbers are expected from
calculations and these would not be convenient to print using the
F field. FORTRAN supports an exponential form of input or output,
the E field. It is written in the FORMAT specification as:

$$k \text{ E } m.n$$

where k specifies the number of repetitions of the field

m specifies the total width of the field

n specifies the number of decimal places

A number printed in this way contains many extra symbols; blanks
or signs, a decimal point, and the letter E. There are so many of
these that m must be greater than n by at least 7. The printing of
E fields comes out as:

$$s\,0\,.\underbrace{ddd....dd}_{\substack{\text{n digits} \\ \text{mantissa}}} \text{E} \underbrace{sdd}_{\text{exponent}}$$

where s is a sign and d are digits. It can be seen that there are
$n + 7$ printed symbols. To allow for blanks between E fields and for
three digit exponents which may sometimes occur, a difference of 10
between m and n is practical.

EXAMPLES: Using a field E15.5, the following numbers would be
printed as shown.

number	printed output
3×10^{10}	$\emptyset.3\emptyset\emptyset\emptyset\emptyset E\ 11$
16.35×10^{-4}	$\emptyset.1635\emptyset E-\emptyset 2$
-7.32×10^{24}	$-\emptyset.732\emptyset\emptyset E\ 25$
-4.28×10^{-15}	$-\emptyset.428\emptyset\emptyset E-14$

As with F fields, FORTRAN allows some slight variations on the exact alignment of input data. First of all the information which is to be read in E form can be moved about within the field of m spaces, and as long as the decimal print and exponent are given no trouble will be encountered. Therefore the number 3×10^{10} could be read in by the statements:

        READ(5,21)X
     21 FORMAT(E15.5)

in several ways including:

        $\emptyset.3\emptyset\emptyset\emptyset\emptyset E\ 11$
        3.$\emptyset$E1$\emptyset$
           3.E1$\emptyset$

The letter E can be left out as long as the sign of the exponent (+ or -) is included:

     3.$\emptyset$+1$\emptyset$
         3.+1$\emptyset$

The decimal point can also be left out, but then it is assumed to precede the n digits of the mantissa:

        3$\emptyset\emptyset\emptyset\emptyset$E 11
     3$\emptyset\emptyset\emptyset\emptyset$+11

PROBLEM 4.7: Stirling's approximation to the factorial of large numbers is:

$$n! \approx \sqrt{2\pi n}\ \left\{\frac{n}{e}\right\}^{n}$$

(i)   By comparison with the exact evaluation, how accurate is it?
(ii) Write a real function to provide the real factorial of an integer argument. The factorial of small numbers should be

calculated as an integer, then converted to real. If the integer
argument is too large then the factorial is too big to represent
as an integer. In this situation the Stirling approximation should
be used.

FEATURE : READING AND WRITING IN EXPONENTIAL FORMAT

FORTRAN   BASIC

WRITE *(i,j)list*   *line number* INPUT *variables*
READ *(i,j)list*
j FORMAT *(specification)*   The *variables* can be typed in
                                           exponential form

If *specification* includes fields   *line number* PRINT *expressions*
of E conversion, then the corresp-
onding variables in *list* which   The results are printed in expon-
must be real, are written or read   ential format if they are large –
in exponential form.   however this cannot be controlled.

The E field is k E $m.n$

k = number of repetitions of the E field
m = total width of the E field
n = the number of decimal places

This is interpreted strictly as

$$\underbrace{\text{s0.ddd...ddEsdd}}_{\text{m spaces}}$$

    n digits   exponent
    mantissa

s = a sign, or for positive numbers a blank
d = a digit

For input the format can be slightly relaxed:

(i)   The number can be moved about in the field
(ii)   The E can be omitted if the sign (+ or -) is
       given
(iii) The decimal point can be omitted and is then
       assumed to precede n digits of the mantissa

5 Subroutine Subprograms—the SUBROUTINE and CALL statements

The subroutine is a very popular facility supported by all versions of FORTRAN. Although a function subprogram can in theory employ any of the facilities of FORTRAN in operating on its arguments, in practice it is most often used for the obvious purpose of providing a single numerical result as part of an expression. The subroutine is used for more general purposes such as considering and modifying its lists of arguments, or performing input/output operations. The use of FUNCTIONS and subroutines enables a good programmer to simplify his programs by apportioning easily identified tasks within the program. This can greatly simplify and shorten a program if it contains the same calculations at different places. However over-zealous programmers can end up devising a maze of subprograms that is virtually incomprehensible. As always, good programming is clear programming.

A subroutine begins with the SUBROUTINE statement, contains at least one RETURN statement, and has an END statement as its last line. The name and list of arguments are defined in the first statement:

> SUBROUTINE *name*(*dummy variables*)
>
> *name* is the name given to the subprogram, but in this case there is no significance to its spelling; the notion of type (real or integer) does not apply to subroutines.
>
> *dummy variables* is a list of variable names separated by commas. Their type is implied by the spelling.

The SUBROUTINE statement is followed by the body of the subprogram which, using the facilities of FORTRAN, can do such things as manipulate the values of the *dummy variables*, initiate input or output, or call on other subprograms. If arithmetic statement functions are desired they must be defined locally within the subroutine, usually following the SUBROUTINE statement, which is non-executable, and before the first executable statement. More will be said about the preferred order of statements at the beginning of programs in the next chapter.

Any variables which are not specified as *dummy variables* in the SUBROUTINE statement are local to the subroutine; they are not known to other parts of the program. This extremely important concept applies just as it does to functions. It is worth noting that subroutines can use other subroutines (or functions); so too can functions use other functions (or subroutines). The variations are inexhaustible.

Within the subprogram at least one RETURN statement indicates the completion of its operation and the return to the program that called it:

RETURN

The subroutine has an END statement as the last line (or card):

END

Subroutines are used by the CALL statement:

CALL *name(arguments)*

name is the name of the subroutine.

arguments is the list of variables or constants to be operated on by the subroutine, separated by commas. Expressions cannot be used. They must be in one-to-one correspondence by type with the *dummy variables* of subroutine *name*. The subroutine uses these for the *dummy variables*. If a *dummy variable* is assigned a new value or changed in any other way by the subroutine, then the corresponding *argument* must not be a constant or the program will be self-destructive.

EXAMPLE: Functions for rectangular to polar conversion were given earlier. A conversion required the use of two functions. It may be more convenient to use a single subroutine.

The following subroutine converts its real arguments ARG1 and ARG2 from rectangular Cartesian co-ordinates to the equivalent polar form of radius and angle. The converted values replace ARG1 and ARG2. The angle (ARG2) is in radians.

```
      SUBROUTINE POLAR(ARG1,ARG2)
C CONVERT CARTESIAN (ARG1,ARG2) TO
C (RADIUS,ANGLE) WITH ANGLE IN RADIANS
      X=SQRT(ARG1*ARG1+ARG2*ARG2)
      ARG2=ATAN2(ARG2,ARG1)
      ARG1=X
      RETURN
      END
```

It should be noticed that in the conversion an intermediate variable X has been used to store what eventually becomes the value of ARG1. This is necessary because the original value of ARG1 is still required for the next statement which calculates the angle. Only then can the new value replace ARG1.

In a main program or another subprogram a statement like the following could appear:

CALL POLAR(X,Y)

and the subroutine would duly convert X and Y. In the call, variables have been used as arguments and so the subroutine has the desired result. However a call such as

CALL POLAR(1.∅,2.∅)

would quietly destroy the calling program. In designing and using a subroutine it is essential to realize that constants may not be used as arguments corresponding to dummy variables which are modified in the subroutine. Were the subroutine instead

```
      SUBROUTINE POLAR(X,Y,RAD,ANG)
C CONVERT CARTESIAN (X,Y) TO
C POLAR (RAD,ANG) WITH ANG IN RADIANS
      RAD=SQRT(X*X+Y*Y)
      ANG=ATAN2(Y,X)
      RETURN
      END
```

Then a call like

CALL POLAR(1.∅,2.∅,P,Q)

would be acceptable. A programmer has to keep account of these finer points of usage himself. The FORTRAN compiler will not save him and the likely result is wrong answers. Note that in the second case the result can be calculated without intermediate variables to save part of the answer because the result does not replace the given data.

EXAMPLE: The following "main program" calls a subroutine ANGLES to find the three angles A1, A2, and A3 of a triangle whose three sides S1, S2 and S3 are known:

```
C FIND THE OPPOSITE ANGLES A1,A2,A3 OF TRIANGLE S1,S2,S3
C FIRST READ IN THE SIDES S1,S2,S3
      READ(5,2Ø)S1,S2,S3
   2Ø FORMAT(3F1Ø.5)
C CALL SUBROUTINE ANGLES TO FURNISH THE OPPOSITE ANGLES
      CALL ANGLES(S1,S2,S3,A1,A2,A3)
C WRITE OUT THE RESULTS
      WRITE(6,3Ø) S1,A1,S2,A2,S3,A3
   3Ø FORMAT(28H SIDE      OPP.ANGLE DEGREES/3(2F15.5/))
      STOP
      END
```

The subroutine ANGLES should check for impossible triangles, and
it could be:

```
      SUBROUTINE ANGLES(X,Y,Z,A,B,C)
C A SUBROUTINE TO CALCULATE THE ANGLES A,B,C
C IN DEGREES OPPOSITE THE GIVEN SIDES X,Y,Z
C CALCULATE CONVERSION FACTOR FROM RADIANS TO DEGREES
      FACTOR=45./ATAN(1.)
C USE THE LAW OF COSINES TO FIND COS(A)
      COSA=(Y*Y+Z*Z-X*X)/(2.*Y*Z)
C CHECK THAT ABS(COSA) IS NOT GREATER THAN 1
      IF(ABS(COSA).GT.1.)GO TO 9Ø
C FIND A IN DEGREES USING INVERSE COS FUNCTION ACOS
      A=ACOS(COSA)*FACTOR
C USE THE RATIO X/SIN(A)=Y/SIN(B) TO FIND B
      B=ASIN(Y*SQRT(1.-COSA*COSA)/X)*FACTOR
      C=18Ø.-A-B
      RETURN
C COME TO HERE IF TRIANGLE IS IMPOSSIBLE
   9Ø WRITE(6,2Ø)X,Y,Z
   2Ø FORMAT(2ØH IMPOSSIBLE TRIANGLE,3F1Ø.5)
      A=Ø.
      B=Ø.
      C=Ø.
      RETURN
      END
```

A flow diagram for this subroutine is given in Fig. 4.4.   In the
main program given earlier, the CALL to ANGLES uses arguments
S1,S2,S3,A1,A2,A3.   The subroutine in execution will use the
values of S1,S2,S3 as its dummy variables X, Y and Z.   It
calculates the angles A, B and C but in execution these are
dummies for A1,A2 and A3 so that when the subroutine returns
control to the main program, A1, A2 and A3 have been calculated.

```
              FEATURE : SUBROUTINE SUBPROGRAMS

        FORTRAN                              BASIC
```

The structure is: The structure is:

SUBROUTINE *name* (*dummy variables*)   *line number* SUB *name* (*dummy variables*)
  :   :
  :   :
RETURN   *line number* SUBEXIT
  ..   :
  :   :
END   *line number*   SUBEND

name is the name of the subroutine.   *name* is the name of the subroutine.
dummy variables is a list of variable *dummy variables* is a list of variable
names separated by commas which are   names separated by commas which are
used in the subroutine as its argu-   used in the subroutines as its arguments. There need not be any. Any   ments. There need not be any. Any
variable name used in the subroutine   variable used in the subroutine which
which is not used in the *dummy*   is not used in the *dummy variable*
variable list is local to the   list is local to the subroutine.
subroutine.

The subroutine is called by the   The subroutine is called by the
statement   statement

CALL *name* (*arguments*)   *line number* CALL *name* (*arguments*)

arguments is a list of variable names *arguments* is a list of variable names
or constants separated by commas which   or constants separated by commas which
are passed to the subroutine to become   are passed to the subroutine to become
the values of its *dummy variables*.   the values of its *dummy variables*.
Care must be taken never to use con-   Care must be taken never to use constants in positions corresponding to   stants in positions corresponding to
variables that are changed by the   variables that are changed by the
subroutine.   subroutine.
                                         Special arrangements are used for
                                         array names.

The RETURN statement indicates where   The SUBEXIT statement indicates where
the subroutine has finished its task   the subroutine has finished its task
and control is to be returned to the   and control is to be returned to the
calling program; there can be   calling program; there can be
several.   several.

The END statement must be the last   The SUBEND statement must be the last
one of the subprogram.   one of the subprogram.

SUBROUTINE ANGLES (X, Y, Z, A, B, C)

```
                    ┌─────────┐
                   (  START   )
                    └────┬────┘
                         │
                         ▼
                  ┌──────────────┐
                  │  CALCULATE   │
                  │  CONVERSION  │
                  │    FACTOR    │
                  │  RADIANS TO  │
                  │   DEGREES    │
                  └──────┬───────┘
                         │
                         ▼
                  ┌──────────────┐
                  │ FIND COS (A) │
                  │ FROM COSINE  │
                  │     LAW      │
                  └──────┬───────┘
                         │
                         ▼
                       ╱   ╲
              NO     ╱   IS   ╲
        ┌──────────╱  COS (A)  ╲
        │          ╲   LEGAL   ╱
        │            ╲   ?   ╱
        │              ╲   ╱
        │               │ YES
        │               │
        ▼               ▼
  ╱──────────╱    ┌──────────────┐
 ╱   PRINT  ╱     │  CALCULATE   │
╱   ERROR  ╱      │     THE      │
╱ MESSAGE ╱       │ THREE ANGLES │
╱─────────╱       └──────┬───────┘
     │                   │
     ▼                   ▼
 ┌────────┐          ┌────────┐
(  RETURN  )        (  RETURN  )
 └────────┘          └────────┘
```

Fig.4.4. Flow diagram for a subroutine to find the angles in a triangle
given the three sides.

The variables FACTOR and COSA are known only within subroutine
ANGLES.   If these names appeared in the main program or in other
subprograms they would not refer to the same variables - those in
ANGLES are local to the subroutine.

In the CALL statement the three angles must be variables as in
this example because they are replaced within the subroutine.
The three sides could be variables or constants since they are not
modified by the subroutine.   All six arguments must be real.

The functions ACOS and ASIN are not standard in FORTRAN - but they
could be provided by the programmer himself as FUNCTION subprograms
or even arithmetic statement functions:

```
ACOS(Z)=ATAN2(SQRT(1.-Z*Z),Z)
ASIN(Z)=ATAN2(Z,SQRT(1.-Z*Z))
```

PROBLEM 4.8:　Problem 3.6 introduced the trapezoidal rule, and in
Problem 4.2 this was revised to use an arithmetic statement
function for f(x).　Rewrite this program yet again using a subroutine for the integration by the trapezoidal rule and a function
subprogram for f(x).

Simpson's rule gives a better formula for the area under two
adjoining trapezoids, Fig. 4.5.

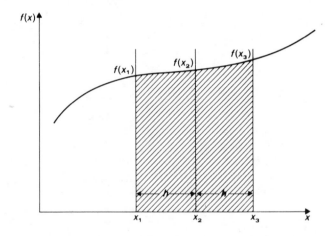

Fig.4.5. Illustrating Simpson's rule.

Here
$$\int_{x_1}^{x_3} f(x)\,dx = \frac{h}{3}\left\{ f(x_1) + 4f(x_2) + f(x_3) \right\}$$

Where segments join, the formula can be rewritten for greater
efficiency.　Write a subroutine to find the area under a curve by
Simpson's rule.　The starting point (x_0), the segment width h, and
the number of segments should be the arguments.　If the number of
segments is odd, this subroutine should call on the trapezoidal
rule to fill in the extra trapezoid.　Again use a function
subprogram for f(x).　Find to 0.1% accuracy:

(i)　　　$0.5 + \dfrac{1}{\sqrt{2\pi}} \displaystyle\int_{0}^{1} e^{-x^2/2}\,dx$

(ii) $\displaystyle\int_0^{\pi/2} \frac{dx}{\sqrt{1 - \dfrac{\sin^2 x}{4}}}$

Compare the step length h required to give this accuracy with the step length needed in Problem 4.2.   What does this mean about the relative accuracy of these methods?

PROBLEM 4.9:   Problem 3.7 introduced a method for solving different-ial equations by numerical integration using Euler's formula.   A more accurate method is the Runge-Kutta procedure, which involves several stages of calculation.   To solve the equation

$$\frac{dy}{dt} = f(y,t)$$

for $y(t_0 + h)$ given $y(t_0)$ calculate first, in order, the quantities

$$k_0 = hf(y_0, t_0)$$

$$k_1 = hf(y_0 + k_0/2 , t_0 + h/2)$$

$$k_2 = hf(y_0 + k_1/2 , t_0 + h/2)$$

$$k_3 = hf(y_0 + k_2 , t_0 + h)$$

and then find the solution

$$y(t_0 + h) = y(t_0) + \frac{1}{6}\left\{k_0 + 2k_1 + 2k_2 + k_3\right\}$$

Write a program to solve first order differential equations by this method.   The main program should read in the starting values, the step size h, and the number of steps desired.   A subroutine should then be used to do the calculation.   Because $f(y,t)$ is used so often, and to make the program general, either a function or a sub-routine should be used for $f(y,t)$.   Solve both the differential equations given in Problem 3.7.   Compare the accuracy and stability of the two methods using various values of h.

PROBLEM 4.10:   Given the Cartesian end coordinates of two line segments write a subroutine or function to find out if they intersect as in Fig. 4.6(a) or do not intersect as in Fig. 4.6(b).   There are many ways of doing this - the clockwise triangle idea can be used or one can actually solve for the intersection of the two lines.

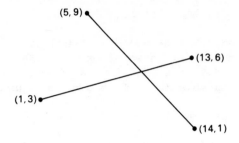

(a) Line segments which intersect.

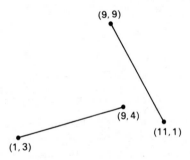

(b) Line segments which do not intersect.

Fig.4.6. Illustrating Problem 4.10. The line segments are specified
by their end co-ordinates.

6 Additional Entries to Subprograms—the ENTRY statement

The ENTRY statement provides a way of entering either a subroutine or function subprogram at more than one place by using different CALL statements or function references. This can be a useful facility but its operation inevitably contains pitfalls which are an open invitation to disaster if the programmer has an incomplete understanding of the use of dummy arguments. The form of the ENTRY statement is

ENTRY *name* (*arguments*)

where *name* is the name of the entry point
      arguments are the dummy arguments for the entry.

The ENTRY statement is not an executable statement. It may appear anywhere in a function or subroutine except in the range of a DO loop. Obviously a subroutine must not call itself, and so a subroutine may not call one of its own entries.

When a CALL or function reference is made to the entry *name*, control passes to the function or subroutine at the ENTRY statement. There must be the usual one-to-one correspondence by type and position between the calling arguments and the dummy arguments of the ENTRY statement. These need not bear any relationship to the subroutine or function arguments or to those of any other entry. When the entry point is called, its dummy arguments are set to the values of the arguments of the CALL throughout the function or subroutine; this is useful but caution is required.

EXAMPLE: One use of multiple entries is to initialize constants within a subroutine. Suppose a subroutine RECT for conversion of polar to rectangular Cartesian co-ordinates is to be used for angles given in either degrees or radians. Entry points are provided so that it can be initialized or switched.

```
      SUBROUTINE RECT(RAD,ANG)
C SUBROUTINE TO CONVERT POLAR (RAD,ANG)
C TO RECTANGULAR (X,Y), THE RESULT REPLACING
C (RAD,ANG). RADIANS OR DEGREES MUST FIRST
C BE SPECIFIED THROUGH ENTRIES RADIAN OR
C DEGREE.  THEY CAN LATER BE SWITCHED.
      X=RAD*COS(ANG*CONST)
      ANG=RAD*SIN(ANG*CONST)
      RAD=X
      RETURN
C ENTRY TO SPECIFY ANG IN RADIANS
      ENTRY RADIAN
      CONST=1.Ø
      RETURN
C ENTRY TO SPECIFY ANG IN DEGREES
      ENTRY DEGREE
      CONST=ATAN(1.Ø)/45.Ø
      RETURN
      END
```

Before using a CALL RECT, either DEGREE or RADIAN must be called to define the value of CONST. A later call can switch the value of CONST.

If multiple entries are used in a function, the operation is more complicated. There must always be at least one argument. The type of a function name is implied by its spelling; so too is the type of an entry and these need not be the same. However misuse of the function or its entry could cause a real value to be returned in an integer variable - not a desirable thing because this is not the same as conversion to an integer. The result would just be rubbish. Similarly the reverse could happen. In returning from the function the value of the function is the most recent one assigned to either the function or one of its entries. This is best illustrated by examples.

EXAMPLES: calling program   subprogram
                   .
                   .
                   .
        I=NUMB(1)   FUNCTION NUMB(K)
        J=MUMB(I)   NUMB=2**K
                                     RETURN
                                     ENTRY MUMB(I)
                                     RETURN
                                     END

Here NUMB returns the value 2 to I, and MUMB also returns the
same value - it has not used its argument nor has it defined a
value for MUMB as might be expected. However a previous call
defined NUMB and this is sufficient.

```
        calling program                 subprogram
              ⋮

        I=NUMB(2)                        FUNCTION ZUMB(K)
        Q=ZUMB(I)                        RETURN
              ⋮                          ENTRY NUMB(K)
              ⋮                          NUMB=2**K
                                         RETURN
                                         END
```

This is a not very practical example illustrating misuse of an
entry point. This program returns correctly a value of 4 to I but
rubbish to Q.

7 Supplementary Problems

PROBLEM 4.11: Various earlier problems were concerned with methods
for evaluating e^x. Write a function to evaluate e^x and compare
its performance with the built-in function EXP.

PROBLEM 4.12: The integral

$$\frac{1}{\sqrt{2\pi}} \int_{-\infty}^{x} e^{-x^2/2} dx$$

is of great importance in statistics and can only be evaluated
numerically. Special cases of this were used to illustrate
numerical integration in earlier problems. Write a function to
evaluate it in the general case.

PROBLEM 4.13: Write a function to evaluate the Bessel function of
the first kind of order n:

$$J_n(x) = x^n \sum_{m=0}^{\infty} \frac{(-1)^m x^{2m}}{2^{2m+n} m! (m+n)!}$$

PROBLEM 4.14: Write a function to evaluate the Gamma   function

$$\Gamma(x) = \int_{0}^{\infty} e^{-t} t^{\alpha-1} dt$$

Because

$$\Gamma(\alpha+1) \ = \ \alpha\Gamma(\alpha)$$

it is not necessary to integrate to infinity. The calculation will resemble the evaluation of a factorial. Indeed

$$\Gamma(k+1) \ = \ k!$$

if k is an integer.

PROBLEM 4.15: Write a subroutine which, given two sets of integer co-ordinates on a straight line, evaluates the equation of the line in the form

$$ax \ + \ by \ + \ c \ = \ 0$$

with a = 1 where possible.

PROBLEM 4.16: Minimization (or maximization) of functions is an important numerical problem in many applications. To minimize $f(x)$, one seeks the place where

$$f'(x) \ = \ 0$$

Occasionally the function will be one whose derivatives can be expressed analytically. In such a situation the Newton-Raphson iteration can be used.

Find the position and value of the minimum of

$$f(x) \ = \ x^4 \ + \ 2x^3 \ - \ x^2 \ - \ 2x \ + \ 3$$

5 Arrays, Subscripts and Storage

1 Introduction

Subscripted variables are of great importance in mathematics and computing alike. Consequently the FORTRAN facilities for defining and using array variables with up to three subscripts are widely used in most calculations of any size. To use these effectively it is vital to be familiar with the concepts of arrays and subscripts, and with the mathematical equivalents.

Until this chapter, the use of a variable has been confined to a single value at one time; these have been scalar variables. With array variables, quantities which are related can be stored at the same time under a single variable name, and used by referring to their subscripts. For example, the number of people living in a house could be called IFOLK and have an integer value. However, suppose there were a row of houses, say 8 of them as in Fig. 5.1. It would be rather tedious to give different variable names to the number of people in each house. However if IFOLK were a subscripted variable, then it would be possible to refer to the number of people in the first house as IFOLK(1), in the second as IFOLK(2), and so on. Working with the figures then becomes relatively easy. To find the total number in the row of houses, one would write something like:

```
      ISUM=Ø
      DO 22 K=1,8
      ISUM=ISUM+IFOLK(K)
   22 CONTINUE
```

Here, the sum is accumulated in the DO-loop as the subscript K is varied, until ISUM holds the result when the DO is satisfied. The subscripted variable IFOLK represents an ordered list of integer quantities; in FORTRAN it is called an integer array.

Other related arrays could be defined, for example the total annual income of each family as shown in Fig. 5.1. WAGES could be a real array containing these incomes still in the same order, and so a program which finds the household with the largest total income might be:

```
      IHOUS=1
      DO 56 K=2,8
      IF(WAGES(K).GT.WAGES(IHOUS))IHOUS=K
   56 CONTINUE
```

At the end, the house number is in IHOUS. What happens if the
largest income is equal in two houses?

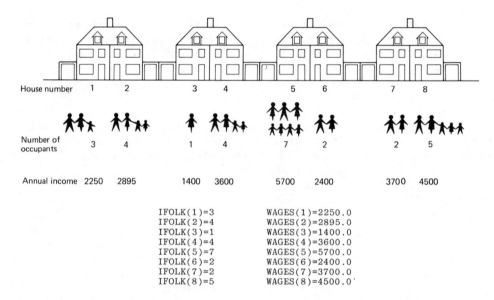

House number	1	2		3	4		5	6		7	8
Number of occupants	3	4		1	4		7	2		2	5
Annual income	2250	2895		1400	3600		5700	2400		3700	4500

```
      IFOLK(1)=3        WAGES(1)=2250.0
      IFOLK(2)=4        WAGES(2)=2895.0
      IFOLK(3)=1        WAGES(3)=1400.0
      IFOLK(4)=4        WAGES(4)=3600.0
      IFOLK(5)=7        WAGES(5)=5700.0
      IFOLK(6)=2        WAGES(6)=2400.0
      IFOLK(7)=2        WAGES(7)=3700.0
      IFOLK(8)=5        WAGES(8)=4500.0
```

Fig. 5.1. The inhabitants of Anystreet showing how many occupy each of the eight
houses and the total family incomes. The numbers of inhabitants are arranged in
the integer array IFOLK and the incomes in the real array WAGES.

In a similar manner a table of values can be held in an array of
two dimensions and referred to using two subscripts. The birth
rate, in live births per 1000 of population per annum might be
broken down into regular geographical areas and a real array BIRTH
used to hold the values, as in Fig. 5.2. If the mean rate over the
whole area were sought, then the FORTRAN statements to provide it
could be

```
      SUM=0.0
      DO 25 K=1,5
      DO 25 L=1,6
      SUM=SUM+BIRTH(K,L)
   25 CONTINUE
      AVG=SUM/30.0
```

after which the mean birth rate is AVG.

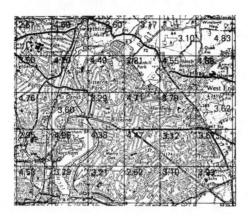

BIRTH(1,1)	BIRTH(1,2)	BIRTH(1,3)	BIRTH(1,4)	BIRTH(1,5)	BIRTH(1,6)
2.67	4.69	3.60	3.17	3.10	4.83
BIRTH(2,1)	BIRTH(2,2)	BIRTH(2,3)	BIRTH(2,4)	BIRTH(2,5)	BIRTH(2,6)
3.50	4.20	4.49	2.81	4.55	4.85
BIRTH(3,1)	BIRTH(3,2)	BIRTH(3,3)	BIRTH(3,4)	BIRTH(3,5)	BIRTH(3,6)
4.76	3.60	3.29	4.71	3.79	3.62
BIRTH(4,1)	BIRTH(4,2)	BIRTH(4,3)	BIRTH(4,4)	BIRTH(4,5)	BIRTH(4,6)
2.95	4.96	4.38	4.47	3.12	3.51
BIRTH(5,1)	BIRTH(5,2)	BIRTH(5,3)	BIRTH(5,4)	BIRTH(5,5)	BIRTH(5,6)
4.53	3.79	3.21	2.52	3.10	3.93

Fig. 5.2. The birth rate per 1000 of population of Anywhere arranged
in the real array BIRTH.

Similarly, arrays of three subscripts are possible. In FORTRAN it
is helpful to know how arrays are arranged in the computer memory,
and using this knowledge some very useful techniques of storage
utilization can be developed. The rules for using arrays and subscripts and the FORTRAN facilities for using them are elaborated in
the sections which follow.

2   Subscripted Variables – the DIMENSION statement

The FORTRAN programmer states clearly his intention to make use of
subscripted variables in a program by first declaring them in a
DIMENSION statement. It is usual for the DIMENSION statements to be
grouped at the beginning of the program; often they must be there*.

The recommended order of statements at the beginning of programs will be spelled out
later. For now put DIMENSION first and then arithmetic statement function definitions.

In the DIMENSION statement variables are named with constant subscripts which state the working size of the arrays.

   An array of one dimension is the equivalent of a vector.   The
statement

       DIMENSION A(3)

defines an array A of one dimension with three members or elements.
The individual members of the array can be accessed by means of
subscripts.   In FORTRAN

       A(2)

is the second of the three elements.   The programmer can consider
his array to be either a row or column vector according to how he
uses it:

$$\begin{pmatrix} A(1) \\ A(2) \\ A(3) \end{pmatrix} \quad or \quad (A(1)\ A(2)\ A(3))$$

In Fig. 5.1 the arrays IFOLK and WAGES would require a DIMENSION
statement such as

       DIMENSION IFOLK(8),WAGES(8)

In a FORTRAN program, the income per inhabitant of the fifth house
could be derived in an arithmetic statement such as

       AVER=WAGES(5)/FLOAT(IFOLK(5))

Note the use of the FLOAT function to avoid mixed mode arithmetic.

   Similarly an array of two dimensions is the equivalent of a matrix.
The statement

       DIMENSION JR(3,3)

defines an integer array JR which would normally be considered
arranged as the matrix:

$$\begin{pmatrix} JR(1,1) & JR(1,2) & JR(1,3) \\ JR(2,1) & JR(2,2) & JR(2,3) \\ JR(3,1) & JR(3,2) & JR(3,3) \end{pmatrix}$$

The real array BIRTH as represented in Fig. 5.2 would require a DIMENSION statement to define it:

    DIMENSION BIRTH(5,6)

and a program to find the average birth rate over the entire area was given earlier.

FORTRAN also supports arrays of three dimensions. If a three dimensional real array XRAY of dimensions 4 x 5 x 6 were desired, then it could be defined by the statement

    DIMENSION XRAY(4,5,6)

Several arrays can be declared in a single DIMENSION statement. A group of arrays could have space reserved by one statement like:

    DIMENSION A(3),IFOLK(8),WAGES(8),JR(5,6),XRAY(4,5,6)

The general form of the DIMENSION statement is then

$$\text{DIMENSION} \quad \begin{matrix} array \\ name \end{matrix} \begin{pmatrix} \text{constant} \\ \text{subscripts} \end{pmatrix} , \quad \begin{matrix} array \\ name \end{matrix} \begin{pmatrix} \text{constant} \\ \text{subscripts} \end{pmatrix} , \quad \cdots$$

The maximum number of subscripts is three.

Once an array has been declared in a DIMENSION statement, it can be used like any other variable in most statements of FORTRAN. The DO statement is the important exception - none of the parameters in a DO statement may be array names. It is usual for the array name to be used always with subscripts - but it is allowed to use it without. If this is done, then the array member referred to is the first one, i.e. in the above examples A would refer to A(1), BIRTH would mean BIRTH(1,1) and XRAY used alone means XRAY(1,1,1).

Two forms of confusion about arrays cause common FORTRAN errors. The first of these arises when an arithmetic expression is intended to include multiplication but the * has been left out - a perfectly natural mistake. If there are brackets nearby FORTRAN could mistake the expression for either a function or an array. The statements

    DEATH=WAGES(IFIX(SIN))
and
    DEATH=WAGES*(IFIX(SIN))

mean very different things. The first is either an incorrect array reference or a function reference depending on whether WAGES was mentioned in a DIMENSION statement or not. If not, FORTRAN will expect to find a function called WAGES.

Similarly any use of subscripts will cause confusion if the DIMENSION information was not given. The statement

X=THING(I,J)

could refer either to an array or a function called THING; the program must contain either a DIMENSION statement or a function definition. Otherwise FORTRAN will expect a FUNCTION subprogram to be given.

EXAMPLE: The following incomplete program prepares a table of tenth order binomial coefficients in the array ICOEFF, using an integer function NCR for $_n C_r$, such as would be a solution to Problem 4.5(i). ICOEFF is therefore an array which must be given in a DIMENSION statement. NCR is not an array, but a function of two variables. There are 11 binomial coefficients required; $_{10} C_0$ is stored in ICOEFF(1), $_{10} C_1$ in ICOEFF(2), and so on.

```
      DIMENSION ICOEFF(11)
      DO 34 IR=1,11
      ICOEFF(IR)=NCR(10,IR-1)
   34 CONTINUE
```

For efficiency, it would be useful to notice that

$$_n C_r = {_n C_{n-r}}$$

and so the program could be rewritten

```
      DIMENSION ICOEFF(11)
      DO 34 IR=1,6
      ICOEFF(IR)=NCR(10,IR-1)
   34 CONTINUE
      DO 35 IR=7,11
      IRR=12-IR
      ICOEFF(IR)=ICOEFF(IRR)
   35 CONTINUE
```

This example raises the question of how complicated a subscript is allowed to be. In the second version, the program takes some trouble to avoid using the subscripted form ICOEFF(12-IR), because it would be incorrect. In FORTRAN the allowed expressions for subscripts are limited to fairly simple forms. First of all a subscript must be an integer expression which gives a result between 1 and the size specified in the DIMENSION statement.   The most complicated expression allowed is:

unsigned integer constant	*	unsigned integer variable	$\pm$	integer constant

The entire list of allowed forms, with valid and invalid examples, is given below:

unsigned integer constant	such as A(4)	but not A(-4) and not A(∅)

unsigned integer variable	such as A(I)	but not A(-I)

unsigned
integer $\pm$ integer   such as ICOEFF(IR-6) but not ICOEFF(6+IR)
variable   constant

unsigned   unsigned
integer   *   integer   such as ARAY(3*J)   but not ARAY(-3*J)
constant   variable   and not ARAY(J*3)

unsigned   unsigned
integer   *   integer $\pm$ integer
constant   variable   constant

such as TWINS(3*K+4,2*J-1)

but not QUEUE(1∅-2*K)
and not QUEUE(-4*L+5)

These restrictions often mean that a desired subscript is not allowed by the rules. In the example of binomial coefficents, it would have been convenient to say

ICOEFF(IR)=ICOEFF(12-IR)

which is not permitted. The usual way of surmounting this obstacle is to define the desired subscript separately in an arithmetic statement as was done in the example:

```
        IRR=12-IR
        ICOEFF(IR)=ICOEFF(IRR)
```

The only additional information required to be able to write
programs using arrays is how to use them in READ and WRITE statements.
The possibilities are described in detail in a later section;   however
to read and write arrays of one dimension is quite easy.   If the array
name is used in the input/output *list*, then the whole array is written
and of course adequate FORMAT provisions must be made.*

EXAMPLES: The binomial coefficients could be printed by the statements

```
        WRITE(6,37)ICOEFF
     37 FORMAT(1X,11I6)
        STOP
        END
```

(which completes the example program except for the function NCR,
which is a solution to Problem 4.5(i)).

The printing could be arranged on three lines with the first a
caption by the statements:

```
        WRITE(6,37)ICOEFF
     37 FORMAT(36H BINOMIAL COEFFICIENTS OF 1ØTH ORDER/(6I1Ø
        STOP
        END
```

PROBLEM 5.1:   Using the information about the inhabitants of
   Anystreet in Fig. 5.1, write a program which

   (i)   finds the families whose incomes per inhabitant are the
          highest, lowest, and nearest the mean.

   (ii)   finds the best-off and worst-off families assuming that the
          children cost half as much as adults to maintain,

   (iii) rearranges the arrays so that the best-off family lives in
          number 1, the next in number 2, and so on.

Arrays can also be used in the *list* part of the free format READ and PRINT statements
described in Section 3.5.

FEATURE : SUBSCRIPTED VARIABLES

FORTRAN   BASIC

The program must declare every variable   The program may declare variables in the
in a DIMENSION or type statement: DIM statement

DIMENSION $\dfrac{array}{name}$ $\left(\dfrac{constant}{subscripts}\right)$, ...   line number DIM $\dfrac{array}{name}$ $\left(\dfrac{constant}{subscripts}\right)$, ...

                                           If not declared, the size is assumed to
                                           be 10 in each dimension.

The maximum number of constant sub-   The maximum number of constant subscripts is three. These define the   scripts is three. These define array
array size.   size.

The *array* name can then be used,   The *array* name can be used with
normally with *subscripts*, in many   *subscripts* in any BASIC statement which
statements of FORTRAN but not all.   allows expressions
The notable exception is the DO
statement.

The *subscripts* must be integers and   *Subscripts* can be any expression, but
limited to the range from 1 to the   their integer part is used and must be
array size.   limited to the range from 1 to the *array*
                                           size.

Subscripts can only be certain
expressions:

unsigned   *unsigned*
integer or   *integer*
constant   *variable*

unsigned
integer $\pm$ *integer*
variable   *constant*

unsigned   *unsigned*
integer *   *integer*
constant   *variable*

unsigned   *unsigned*
integer *   *integer* $\pm$ *integer*
constant   *variable*   *constant*

PROBLEM 5.2:   The steady state distribution of temperature in a bar
obeys a partial differential equation

$$\frac{\partial^2 T}{\partial x^2} = k \frac{\partial u}{\partial t}$$

which takes account of variations along the length of the bar
(Fig. 5.3) in the temperature T and also the removal of heat
$\frac{k \partial u}{\partial t}$

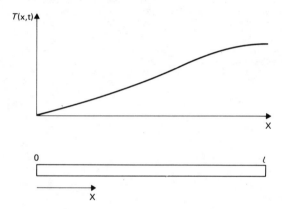

Fig. 5.3. Temperature distribution in a thin bar.

Suppose the bar is of unit length and cooled so that

$$\frac{\partial^2 T}{\partial x^2} = T + 100$$

with the ends of the bar held at constant temperature of $120^{\circ}C$ at
x = 0 and $200^{\circ}C$ at x = ℓ.   This equation has an analytic solution
for these given end conditions:

$$T(x) = 93.203e^{x} + 126.796e^{-x} - 100$$

and this can be used as a standard for comparing the numerical
solutions required in this problem.

To calculate the solution on a computer, it is usual to divide
the bar into segments and to devise a difference equation which
approximates or "models" the partial differential equation.
Suppose three adjacent pieces of the bar each of length h are
considered as in Fig. 5.4.   In this region two approximations can
be made to $\frac{\partial T}{\partial x}$:

Midway between T_k and T_{k-1} $\frac{\partial T}{\partial x} \approx \frac{T_k - T_{k-1}}{h}$

and between T_{k+1} and T_k $\frac{\partial T}{\partial x} \approx \frac{T_{k+1} - T_k}{h}$

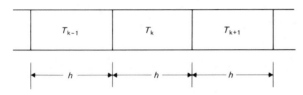

Fig. 5.4. Three segments of the bar.

Using the difference between these gives an estimate of $\frac{\partial^2 T}{\partial x^2}$ at T_k
so that the model of

$$\frac{\partial^2 T}{\partial x^2} = T + 100$$

is $$\frac{T_{k+1} - 2T_k + T_{k-1}}{h^2} = T_k + 100$$

or $$T_k = \frac{1}{2 + h^2} \left\{ T_{k+1} + T_{k-1} - 100h^2 \right\}$$

To carry out a solution, guess at a temperature distribution and calculate from it a new one using the model equation, taking account of the end conditions. Repeat the calculation of new temperatures from old over and over again (this is called iteration) Eventually a solution will be achieved which is accurate if suffic- ient segments have been used and if sufficient iterations have been carried out to enable the solution to converge towards an answer. In a simple case, such as this one it may seem strange to go to so much effort to solve an equation whose analytic solution is known.   However in many more complex problems the analytic solution can be very difficult (or impossible) whereas the numerical solution is based on the same principles.

(a)   Write a program to solve this equation.   Investigate its accuracy as a function of h and its convergence as a function of both h and the number of iterations.

Now suppose a different iteration is used:

$$T_k^{new} = (1-\omega) T_k^{old} + \frac{\omega}{2 + h^2} \left\{ T_{k+1}^{old} + T_{k-1}^{new} - 100h^2 \right\}$$

It should be obvious that the case $\omega = 1$ describes the same process as above, and that if $0 < \omega < 1$ the solution will progress at a slow rate of convergence; this is called under-relaxation.   If $\omega > 1$ the process is accelerated; this is called over-relaxation and could make the solution unstable.

(b)   Investigate the use of under- and over-relaxation and its effect on convergence accuracy, and stability.

3 Defining Values in Advance—the DATA statement

Up to this point, data used by programs has been entered by READ statements or defined in arithmetic statements. This is convenient for reasonable numbers of scalar variables, but with large arrays it could be very inconvenient. The DATA statement of FORTRAN allows initial values to be set up and assigned to variables before the program is actually executed. The DATA statement simply names the variables to be defined and gives them values in the form

DATA *list* / *values* /, *list* / *values* /, ...

EXAMPLES:

DATA PIE/3.14159265/,E/2.71828182845/

assigns the real value 3.14159265 to PIE and 2.71828182845 to E, which are assumed to be scalar.

DATA I,J,K,L/17,23,29,31/

assigns the integer values 17, 23, 29 and 31 to integer variables I, J, K, and L.

As might be expected the variables given in the *list* and the constants given as their *values* must be in one-to-one correspondence according to type and position. Therefore the statement

DATA X,I,Y,J/1.3,3,7.9,11/

is correct whereas

DATA JOHN,FRED,MARY,LINDA/1,2,3,4/

is incorrect because the real variable FRED is assigned an integer value.

Subscripted variables can appear in the DATA statement. If a constant subscript is used, then only the specified array member is defined, as in

DIMENSION BLOCK(3Ø)
DATA I,BLOCK(2Ø),X/1,3.14,15.Ø/

in which BLOCK(2Ø) is given the value 3.14. If an array name is given without subscripts, then the whole array must be defined, as in

```
      DIMENSION IFOLK(8),WAGES(8)
      DATA IFOLK/3,4,1,4,7,2,2,5/
      DATA WAGES/2250.,2895.,1400.,3600.,5700.,2400.,
     1 3700.,4500./
```
which defines the arrays used in an earlier example, Fig. 5.1.

A value specification can be repeated to save writing the same values over and over by writing the number of repetitions of a value and an asterisk before the repeated value. Thus to give an array ONES identical values of 1.0, write

```
      DIMENSION ONES(5)
      DATA ONES/5*1.0/
```

an entire unit matrix is specified by

```
      DIMENSION UNIT(4,4)
      DATA UNIT/1.,4*0.,1.,4*0.,1.,4*0.,1./
```
to be

$$\begin{pmatrix} 1. & 0. & 0. & 0. \\ 0. & 1. & 0. & 0. \\ 0. & 0. & 1. & 0. \\ 0. & 0. & 0. & 1. \end{pmatrix}$$

However a peculiarity arises with arrays of two dimensions; the values are defined in *column* order which makes no difference to the unit matrix above but is important in most cases. In a later section it will be seen that this is a consequence of the arrangement of arrays in the computer memory. For present purposes it must be noted that the values assigned to an array of two dimensions by a DATA statement must be given in column order, i.e down the first column, then down the second and so on, Therefore the DATA statement in

```
      DIMENSION ARAY(3,3)
      DATA ARAY /1.0,2.0,3.0,4.0,5.0,6.0,7.0,8.0,9.0/
```

defines the matrix

$$\begin{pmatrix} 1.0 & 4.0 & 7.0 \\ 2.0 & 5.0 & 8.0 \\ 3.0 & 6.0 & 9.0 \end{pmatrix}$$

although the transposed result might be expected (and catch a careless programmer unawares). More will be said about this later.

It must be emphasised that the values assigned in the DATA statement are only initial values. If any of these values are changed later on in the program, the new value takes effect just as with any variable. There is no automatic way of recovering initial values established in the DATA statement once modifications have occured.

In a later chapter, types of variables other than real or integer will be introduced, and these can also have their initial values assigned by DATA statements. There is an exception to the use of DATA statements which is explained in Section 5 of this Chapter - they cannot be used with variables assigned to the blank COMMON area.

Again with the DATA statement it is usual to follow a particular order of statements at the beginning of a program; it is best to follow the recommended order because on many computers it is obligatory. Although further order-dependent statements follow in later sections, the order of statements known so far should be:

In a main program   DIMENSION
                                 DATA
                                 Arithmetic statement function definitions

In a subprogram   FUNCTION or SUBROUTINE
                                 DIMENSION
                                 DATA
                                 Arithmetic statement function definitions

Note that a special section on the use of arrays in subroutines follows later in this chapter. It would be wise not to attempt to pass arrays as subroutine arguments at this stage.

PROBLEM 5.3: Use a DATA statement to define the values of birth rate over the geographical area shown in Fig. 5.2. Find

(i)   The mean and standard deviation of the 30 different birth rates.

(ii) The co-ordinates and values of all areas whose birth rate is different from the mean by more than the standard deviation.

4 Printing of Arrays—implied DO loops

The names of array variables can be used in WRITE (and READ) statements in several ways. The obvious one would be the use of a constant subscript, as in

```
      DIMENSION BUNK(3)
      DATA BUNK/7.7,15.0,8.1/
      WRITE(6,20)BUNK(1),BUNK(2),BUNK(3)
   20 FORMAT(1X,3F6.2)
      STOP
      END
```

which would produce the line

```
 7.70 15.00  8.10
```

However, as in the DATA statement the same effect can be achieved by
naming the array without subscripts, as in

```
      WRITE(6,20)BUNK
```

which would produce the identical result. Simply including the
array variable in the output *list* of a WRITE statement without subscripts causes the entire array to be printed. In planning the
associated FORMAT, account has to be taken of the size and type of
the array so that the correspondence between the output *list* and the
FORMAT *specification* is maintained. The identical facility is
available for input, so that the statements

```
      DIMENSION JILL(5)
      READ(5,31)JILL
   31 FORMAT(I4)
```

expect the 5 values for the integer array JILL to be provided on 5
different lines in FORMAT I4.

   The same complication for arrays of two dimensions occurs as in
the DATA statement. FORTRAN was originally designed to read and
write arrays in column order and although the designers may have
had second thoughts subsequently, it is now too late to change it.
Suppose the 3x3 array IQ has values

$$\begin{pmatrix} 100 & 110 & 120 \\ 130 & 140 & 150 \\ 160 & 170 & 180 \end{pmatrix}$$

then just as the DATA statement had to be specified in column order,
i.e.

```
      DATA  IQ/100,130,160,110,140,170,120,150,180/
```

so in READ or WRITE statements FORTRAN will use the same order, so

FEATURE : ASSIGNMENT OF VALUES TO VARIABLES

There are major differences between the DATA statements

of FORTRAN and BASIC

FORTRAN	BASIC

The DATA statement assignes values to variables

DATA *list/values/,list/values/,...*

list is a series of variable names separated by commas

values is a series of numeric constants separated by commas which are initial *values* assigned to *list*. There must be a one-to-one correspondence by type and position between *list* and *values*.

Arrays can be defined in three ways:

  (i) single elements with constant subscripts

    DATA A(2)/51.2/

 (ii) the entire array, named without a subscript

    DIMENSION A(3)
    DATA A/13.4,51.2,16.7/

(iii) All or part of the array with a variable subscrip given in an implied DO-loop (see Chapter 5, Section 4)

    DIMENSION IRAY(3∅)
    DATA(IRAY(K),K=6,1∅)/17,19,23,29,31/

The DATA statement specifies initial values which cease to apply if the variables are redefined.

The DATA statement cannot be used to define variables in unlabelled COMMON (see Chapter 5, Section 5)

See also Chapter 6 for the use of other variable types.

The DATA statement is one which must often appear in a particular order of statements at the beginning of programs. See Chapter 5, Section 7.

BASIC column:

The DATA statement sets up a block of defined values

line number DATA *values*

Successive DATA statements add to the block

The READ statement takes values from the DATA block and assigns them to variables
line number READ *variables*

Successive READ statements assign values to the named variables one by one from the DATA block.

A RESTORE statement returns to the beginning of the DATA block for subsequent reading.

line number RESTORE

that
```
      WRITE(6,1ØØ)IQ
 1ØØ FORMAT(1X3I1Ø)
```

will produce the printed result

```
       1ØØ         13Ø         16Ø
...............................
       11Ø         14Ø         17Ø
...............................
       12Ø         15Ø         18Ø
...............................
```

which unfortunately prints the columns on paper as if they were rows. The novice may be forgiven if he confuses his FORTRAN with his mathematics; great care is necessary to avoid situations where the transpose of a matrix has been used in error because of this. Similarly the READ statement

```
      READ(5,99)IQ
 99 FORMAT(9I4)
```

will expect all of the array IQ to be given on one line (or card) but in column order.

Fortunately there are ways around this which most experienced programmers adopt as a matter of reflex. One could always write

```
      DO 66 K=1,3
      DO 66 L=1,3
      WRITE(6,67)IQ(K,L)
 66 CONTINUE
 67 FORMAT(1XI4)
```

which of course prints the contents in row order, that is IQ(1,1) then IQ(1,2), then IQ(1,3), then IQ(2,1) and so on, but they are each on separate lines. The two nested DO-loops are given explicitly to control the order of printing. FORTRAN also allows what are called implied DO-loops in DATA, READ, or WRITE statements which allow the kind of printing which is desired. For defining and printing the demonstration array IQ, one could have

```
      DIMENSION IQ(3,3)
      DATA((IQ(K,L),L=1,3),K=1,3)/1ØØ,11Ø,12Ø
     1,13Ø,14Ø,15Ø,16Ø,17Ø,18Ø/
      WRITE(6,3Ø)((IQ(K,L),L=1,3),K=1,3)
 3Ø FORMAT(1X3I1Ø)
```

which would produce the array in the usual layout on paper, i.e.

```
        1ØØ         11Ø         12Ø
. . . . . . . . . . . . . . . . . . . . . . . . . . .
        13Ø         14Ø         15Ø
. . . . . . . . . . . . . . . . . . . . . . . . . . .
        16Ø         17Ø         18Ø
. . . . . . . . . . . . . . . . . . . . . . . . . . .
```

which is highly desirable. The same arrangement would apply in a
READ statement

```
      READ(5,99)((IQ(K,L),L=1,3),K=1,3)
   99 FORMAT(9I4)
```

In this case the 9 values would still be expected on one card but in
row order.

   The syntax for implied DO-loops must be exact. In the above
examples all the brackets and commas are required and furthermore
redundant ones cannot be allowed. A set of brackets is required to
enclose the implied loop for each subscript. Within this arrangement a variety of subscripted variables can be used if there is a
loop to refer to them. Thus in the case of one dimension the
following examples are all allowed

```
      DATA(JILL(K),K=4,5)/7,8/
      READ(5,21)(JILL(K),IQ(1,K),K=1,3)
      WRITE(6,24)((JILL(L),IQ(K,L),L=1,3),K=1,3)
      WRITE(6,24)(JILL(K),(IQ(K,L),L=1,3),K=1,3)
```

$$_0C_0$$
$$_1C_0 \qquad _1C_1$$
$$_2C_0 \qquad _2C_1 \qquad _2C_2$$
$$_3C_0 \qquad _3C_1 \qquad _3C_2 \qquad _3C_3$$
$$_4C_0 \qquad _4C_1 \qquad _4C_2 \qquad _4C_3 \qquad _4C_4$$
$$_5C_0 \qquad _5C_1 \qquad _5C_2 \qquad _5C_3 \qquad _5C_4 \qquad _5C_5$$
$$_6C_0 \qquad _6C_1 \qquad _6C_2 \qquad _6C_3 \qquad _6C_4 \qquad _6C_5 \qquad _6C_6$$

Fig. 5.5. Arrangement of binomial coefficients in Pascal's triangle.

PROBLEM 5.4:   The arrangement of binomial coefficients shown in
Fig. 5.5 is called Pascal's triangle.   The entire triangle can be
generated without evaluating any factorials by noticing that

$$_nC_r = \frac{n-r+1}{r} \,_nC_{r-1}$$

i.e. each number is calculated from the one on its left. The first
number in a row is always 1. The second number is calculated from
the first using the formula, and so on. this is a good example of
recurrence – the formula is very easily obtained (try it). In standa
FORTRAN it is difficult to print these numbers as a triangle, but it
is easy to produce them as shown in Fig. 5.6.

Write a program using an array of one dimension to calculate and
print each row in turn, and so print 10 rows of Pascal's triangle.

```
1
1    1
1    2    1
1    3    3    1
1    4    6    4    1
1    5    10   10   5    1
1    6    15   20   15   6    1
etc.
```

Fig. 5.6. FORTRAN scheme for printing Pascal's triangle.

PROBLEM 5.5:   Arrays of two dimensions are often used to represent
the coefficients of systems of linear equations such as

$$a_{11}x_1 + a_{12}x_2 + a_{13}x_3 = y_1 \qquad\qquad (1)$$

$$a_{21}x_1 + a_{22}x_2 + a_{23}x_3 = y_2 \qquad\qquad (2)$$

$$a_{31}x_1 + a_{32}x_2 + a_{33}x_3 = y_3 \qquad\qquad (3)$$

For programming the given coefficents and right hand side would
usually be arranged in arrays, here called A and Y

$$
\begin{array}{cc}
A & Y \\[4pt]
\begin{pmatrix}
a_{11} & a_{12} & a_{13} \\
a_{21} & a_{22} & a_{23} \\
a_{31} & a_{31} & a_{33}
\end{pmatrix}
&
\begin{pmatrix}
y_1 \\
y_2 \\
y_3
\end{pmatrix}
\end{array}
$$

A popular means of solving these equations involves eliminating
variables from equations which can be arranged systematically into
what is called the method of Gaussian elimination. The first step
would be to eliminate variable x_1 from equation (2) by subtracting
row (1) times a_{21}/a_{11} from row (2) to give a new row (2).

The right hand side of the equation is also operated on to give a
new term

$$y_2' = y_2 - (a_{21}/a_{11})y_1$$

Similarly variable x, is eliminated from equation (3) by subtracting row (1) times a_{31}/a_{11} from row (3) to give a new row (3) and
a new right hand side. In this operation a_{11} is called the pivot.
This gives a new set of equations

$$a_{11}x_1 + a_{12}x_2 + a_{13}x_3 = y_1 \qquad (1)$$
$$b_{22}x_2 + b_{23}x_3 = y_2' \qquad (4)$$
$$b_{32}x_2 + b_{33}x_3 = y_3' \qquad (5)$$

The variable x_2 can now be removed from equation (5), using b_{22}
as the pivot, subtracting equation (2) times b_{32}/b_{22} from equation
(5) to give a new equation (6). The equations are now

$$a_{11}x_1 + a_{12}x_2 + a_{13}x_3 = y_1 \qquad (1)$$
$$b_{22}x_2 + b_{23}x_3 = y_2' \qquad (4)$$
$$c_{33}x_3 = y_3'' \qquad (6)$$

If the coefficients were originally arranged in an array A of two
dimensions and the right hand side in an array Y of one dimension,
then the arrays are transformed as the elimination progresses:

$$
\text{A} \qquad\qquad \text{Y}
$$

$$
\text{initially} \quad
\begin{pmatrix}
a_{11} & a_{12} & a_{13} \\
a_{21} & a_{22} & a_{23} \\
a_{31} & a_{32} & a_{33}
\end{pmatrix}
\text{ and }
\begin{pmatrix}
y_1 \\
y_2 \\
y_3
\end{pmatrix}
$$

$$
\text{after stage 1} \quad
\begin{pmatrix}
a_{11} & a_{12} & b_{13} \\
0 & b_{22} & b_{23} \\
0 & b_{32} & b_{33}
\end{pmatrix}
\text{ and }
\begin{pmatrix}
y_1 \\
y_2' \\
y_3'
\end{pmatrix}
$$

and finally
$$\begin{pmatrix} a_{11} & a_{12} & a_{13} \\ 0 & b_{22} & b_{23} \\ 0 & 0 & c_{33} \end{pmatrix} \text{ and } \begin{pmatrix} y_1 \\ y_2' \\ y_3'' \end{pmatrix}$$

If there were N equations, then the algorithm can be generalized:

> For each column K from 1 to N - 1
>> For each row I from K + 1 to N - 1
>>> Operate on Y(I) by
>>> letting Y(I) = Y(I) - Y(K)*A(I,K)/A(K,K)
>>>> And also along the row for J from K to N
>>>> Operate on A(I,J) by
>>>> letting A(I,J) = A(I,J) - A(K,J)*A(I,K)/A(K,K)

The progress of this algorithm is shown frozen at I, J, K in Fig. 5.7

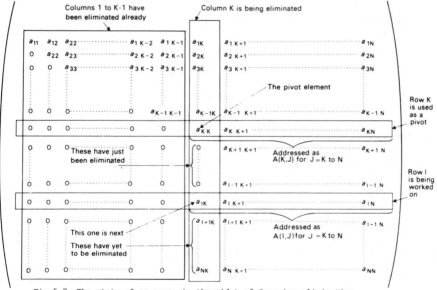

Fig.5.7. The state of an array in the midst of Gaussian elimination.
Row K is used as pivot for the elimination of column K, which has
progressed to row I.

The algorithm as stated above is easily translated directly into
FORTRAN; however, it will not work exactly as stated, because the
first element in each row to be operated on is A(I,K) (when J=K).
Unfortunately the old value of A(I,K) is still required in the

remainder of operations in row I. It is necessary to preserve the original A(I,K) somehow. The usual way is to use a scalar variable, say Z, to hold A(I,K)/A(K,K) for the whole of row K, using the procedures

$$Y(I) = Y(I) - Y(K)*Z$$

and

$$A(I,J) = A(I,J) - A(K,J)*Z$$

This also has some advantages in efficiency since there is less arithmetic and subscripting in the innermost loop.

Once the elimination is complete, the solution to the equation is found by back-substitution:

$$x_3 = y_3''/c_{33}$$
$$x_2 = (y_2' - b_{23}x_3)/b_{22}$$
$$x_1 = (y_1 - a_{12}x_2 - a_{13}x_3)/a_{11}$$

which can be described in the general case of N equations as first:

$$X(N) = Y(N)/A(N,N)$$

and for each row K from N - 1 to 1

$$X(K) = Y(K) - \sum_{J=K+1}^{N} A(K,J)*X(J)/A(K,K)$$

In FORTRAN DO-loops do not run backwards and so an arrangement like

```
NN1=N-1
DO 66 K=1,NN1
KK=N-K
    :
    :
66 CONTINUE
```

to make the counter KK run backwards is necessary.

The entire process for solving equations by Gaussian elimination is illustrated by the flow diagram of Fig. 5.8

Write a FORTRAN program to solve the equations

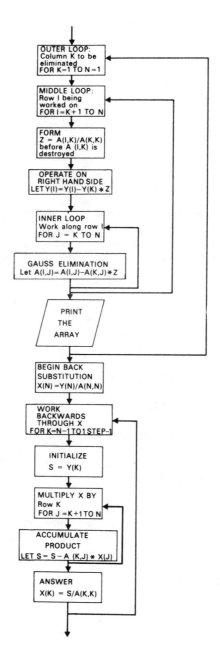

Fig.5.8. Flow diagram for Gaussian elimination and back-substitution.

$$10x_1 - 7x_2 + 3x_3 + 5x_4 = 6$$

$$-6x_1 + 8x_2 - x_3 - 4x_4 = 5$$

$$3x_1 + x_2 + 4x_3 + 11x_4 = 2$$

$$5x_1 - 9x_2 - 2x_3 + 4x_4 = 7$$

by Gaussian elimination. Show the array of coefficients and the right hand side after each stage. Answer $(5,1,-7,1)$

5 Storage Arrangements—the EQUIVALENCE statement

When a FORTRAN program is executed, the memory of the computer holds the complied version of the program and all its variables. The scalar variables which represent single numbers occupy a particular amount of space in the memory which will be called one "location". Array variables occupy more space depending on how large the array was made in the DIMENSION statement which declared it. Not surprisingly, the space reserved for an array of one dimension is in a continuous block in the memory; in Fig. 5.9 a possible storage scheme is shown for a program with the DIMENSION statement

DIMENSION ICOEFF(11)

which also refers to scalar variables named IRR, IR and to the integer constants 1, 11, 10, 6, 7 and 12. In fact this could be the program to calculate and print the binomial coefficients which was used as an example in section 2 of this chapter. In the array ICOEFF, the memory locations are grouped together in 11 successive spaces as might be expected.

For an array of two dimensions, the memory locations used are also blocked together but obviously they must occur either in row or column order. In FORTRAN they occur in columns as shown in Fig. 5.10 for the two dimensional array IQ, defined by

DIMENSION IQ(3,3)
DATA IQ/1ØØ,13Ø,16Ø,11Ø,14Ø,17Ø,12Ø,15Ø,18Ø/

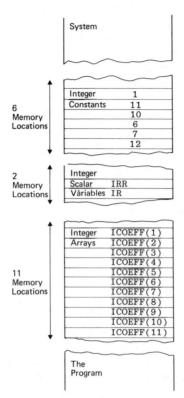

Fig. 5.9. Arrangement of variables in the memory of a typical computer
including the array of one dimension ICOEFF.

1	100	IQ(1,1)	IQQ(1)
2	130	IQ(2,1)	IQQ(2)
3	160	IQ(3,1)	IQQ(3)
4	110	IQ(1,2)	IQQ(4)
5	140	IQ(2,2)	IQQ(5)
6	170	IQ(3,2)	IQQ(6)
7	120	IQ(1,3)	IQQ(7)
8	150	IQ(2,3)	IQQ(8)
9	180	IQ(3,3)	IQQ(9)

9 Memory Locations

Fig. 5.10. Arrangement of the 3 x 3 array IQ in the memory of a typical computer
showing an equivalent storage arrangement for the array of one dimension IQQ.

Another way of describing the storage arrangement is to say that the
first subscript varies most rapidly through memory. Since the
storage arrangement is known, it is easy for the FORTRAN program to
find a given array member in storage. A member IQ(I,J) is found
I + (J-1)*3 locations along the array. This suggests that for every
array of two dimensions there is an equivalent array of one
dimension which could be used in its place. This is so. Although
two subscripts are usually a great convenience, any calculation
involving such an array could be done with one - and sometimes may
have to be as will be seen when discussing subroutines in the next
section. In Fig. 5.10, the location IQ(I,J) is the equivalent of
IQQ(I +(J-1)*3), except of course that J + (K-1)*3 is an illegally
complicated subscript. The two programs listed here side by side
are equivalent:

```
        DIMENSION IQ(3,3)                DIMENSION IQQ(9)
        IVAL=1ØØ                         IVAL=1ØØ
        DO 3Ø I=1,3                      DO 3Ø I=1,3
        DO 3Ø J=1,3                      DO 3Ø J=1,3
        IQ(I,J)=IVAL                     IJ=I+(J-1)*3
        IVAL=IVAL+1Ø                     IQQ(IJ)=IVAL
    3Ø CONTINUE                          IVAL=IVAL+1Ø
                                     3Ø CONTINUE
```

These programs define the array as shown in Fig. 5.10, and of course
in practice a DATA statement would be used where possible. It is
also unlikely that the right hand version would be used out of
choice but in some circumstances there might be no alternative. In
general an array of two dimensions ℓ x m is equivalent to an array
of one dimension ℓ * m; a subscript (I,J) in the former corresponds
to a subscript I + (J-1)*ℓ in the latter.

Similarly a three dimensional array is stored in the order with
its first subscripts varying most rapidly and its third subscript
varying least rapidly. The array defined by

    DIMENSION XRAY(2,3,4)

is stored as shown in Fig. 5.11. The equivalent one dimensional
subscript to (I,J,K) is I + (J-1)*2 +(K-1)*3*4. In general an
ℓ x m x n array is equivalent to a single array of size ℓ * m * n
and a subscript (I,J,K) in the case of three dimensions is
equivalent to a single subscript I +(J-1)*ℓ+(K-1)*m*ℓ.

```
         1   XRAY(1,1,1)
         2   XRAY(2,1,1)
         3   XRAY(1,2,1)
         4   XRAY(2,2,1)
         5   XRAY(1,3,1)
         6   XRAY(2,3,1)
         7   XRAY(1,1,2)
         8   XRAY(2,1,2)
         9   XRAY(1,2,2)
   24   10   XRAY(2,2,2)
Memory  11   XRAY(1,3,2)
Locations 12  XRAY(2,3,2)
        13   XRAY(1,1,3)
        14   XRAY(2,1,3)
        15   XRAY(1,2,3)
        16   XRAY(2,2,3)
        17   XRAY(1,3,3)
        18   XRAY(2,3,3)
        19   XRAY(1,1,4)
        20   XRAY(2,1,4)
        21   XRAY(1,2,4)
        22   XRAY(2,2,4)
        23   XRAY(1,3,4)
        24   XRAY(2,3,4)
```

Fig. 5.11. Arrangement of the 2 x 3 x 4 array XRAY in the
memory of a typical computer.

More complicated equivalences are possible. For example the array
of three dimensions ℓ x m x n is also equivalent to either an array
of two dimensions ℓ x(m * n) or an array of two dimensions (ℓ * m) x n
with appropriately complicated subscripts. If any of the subscripts
can be factored then other combinations are equivalent.

It can often happen in a larger or complicated FORTRAN program that
the programmer works at different times with different arrays, and in
order to save space he wishes to use the same storage for several
arrays. Knowing the arrangements of arrays in storage, he can be
very cunning and have the same space used for arrays of different
dimensions at different times, perhaps even sharing values as will
be tried in Problem 5.6. To make this easy for him, the EQUIVALENCE
statement allows the same space to be given to several arrays which
may have different names, different numbers of subscripts, and even
different type.*

Assuming that real and integer variables use the same space for one "location", all the arrays referred to in this section could be kept in the same space by the statements

DIMENSION ICOEFF(11),IQ(3,3),IQQ(9),XRAY(2,3,4)
EQUIVALENCE (ICOEFF,IQ,IQQ,XRAY)

with the result shown in Fig. 5.12.

ICOEFF(1)	IQ(1,1)	IQQ(1)	XRAY(1,1,1)
ICOEFF(2)	IQ(2,1)	IQQ(2)	XRAY(2,1,1)
ICOEFF(3)	IQ(3,1)	IQQ(3)	XRAY(1,2,1)
ICOEFF(4)	IQ(1,2)	IQQ(4)	XRAY(2,2,1)
ICOEFF(5)	IQ(2,2)	IQQ(5)	XRAY(1,3,1)
ICOEFF(6)	IQ(3,2)	IQQ(6)	XRAY(2,3,1)
ICOEFF(7)	IQ(1,3)	IQQ(7)	XRAY(1,1,2)
ICOEFF(8)	IQ(2,3)	IQQ(8)	XRAY(2,1,2)
ICOEFF(9)	IQ(3,3)	IQQ(9)	XRAY(1,2,2)
ICOEFF(10)			XRAY(2,2,2)
ICOEFF(11)			XRAY(1,3,2)
			XRAY(2,3,2)
			XRAY(1,1,3)
			XRAY(2,1,3)
			XRAY(1,2,3)
			XRAY(2,2,3)
			XRAY(1,3,3)
			XRAY(2,3,3)
			XRAY(1,1,4)
			XRAY(2,1,4)
			XRAY(1,2,4)
			XRAY(2,2,4)
			XRAY(1,3,4)
			XRAY(2,3,4)

Fig. 5.12. Arrangement of arrays of one, two, and three dimensions in memory using an EQUIVALENCE statement. It is assumed here that real and integer locations use the same storage space.

Note that since the arrays are not all the same length, the total space taken is dictated by the largest, XRAY. The programmer is free to refer to any of these arrays at any time by their separate names using the correct number of subscripts. However, since they share the same physical memory space he must be careful that their different uses do not interfere. If he changes XRAY(2,2,1) he is destroying IQQ(4), IQ(1,2) and ICOEFF(4); not only that he is placing in them a real value which will be nonsense if referred to later as an integer. The statements

XRAY(2,2,1)=1.∅

or

XRAY(2,2,1)=1

do not mean the same as

    IQ(1,2)=1

because the integer value 1 does *not* resemble the real value 1.0 in memory.

  The general form of the EQUIVALENCE statement is

    EQUIVALENCE (*variables*), (*variables*),.....

Groups of *variables* enclosed in brackets are defined in this statement to be equivalent. The *variables* can be scalar or array names with or without subscripts. The effect of the EQUIVALENCE statement is to force the named variables to have the same memory location - and the remainder of the arrays line up accordingly. Naturally enough impossible arrangements cannot be allowed and so arrays cannot be broken into pieces. In the given examples, some realignments would be possible such as

    EQUIVALENCE(IQ,IQQ,XRAY),(ICOEFF,XRAY(2,2,2))

which would move the array ICOEFF down so that while it still shares space with XRAY, it does not overlap the arrays IQ and IQQ.

  EQUIVALENCE is another of the order-dependent statements. It must follow the DIMENSION statement but precede the DATA statement. Therefore the rules for order-dependent statements must be brought up to date once more:

Main program

        DIMENSION
        EQUIVALENCE
        DATA
        Arithmetic statement function definitions

Subprogram

        FUNCTION or SUBROUTINE
        DIMENSION
        EQUIVALENCE
        DATA
        Arithmetic statement function definitions

PROBLEM 5.6:   The Crout reduction for factorization of an array into the product of lower and upper triangular forms is an efficient basis either for solving linear equations or for inverting a matrix.   Suppose an n by n array A can be factored so that it is the product of a lower triangular matrix L with an upper triangular matrix U, and that the diagonal of U can consist of ones.   Then

$$A = LU$$

or

$$
\begin{bmatrix}
a_{11} & a_{12} & \cdots & a_{1n} \\
a_{21} & a_{22} & \cdots & a_{2n} \\
\vdots & \vdots & & \vdots \\
a_{n1} & a_{n2} & \cdots & a_{nn}
\end{bmatrix}
=
\begin{bmatrix}
\ell_{11} & 0 & 0 & \cdots & 0 \\
\ell_{21} & \ell_{22} & 0 & \cdots & 0 \\
\vdots & & & & \\
\ell_{n1} & \ell_{n2} & \ell_{n3} & \cdots & \ell_{nn}
\end{bmatrix}
\begin{bmatrix}
1 & u_{12} & u_{13} & \cdots & u_{1n} \\
0 & 1 & u_{23} & \cdots & u_{2n} \\
\vdots & & & & \vdots \\
0 & 0 & 0 & \cdots & 1
\end{bmatrix}
$$

and the means of accomplishing the factorization can be found by inspecting the product LU.   First of all

$$a_{11} = \ell_{11}$$

$$a_{21} = \ell_{21}$$

and so on to define column 1 of L.   Then

$$a_{12} = \ell_{11}u_{12} \quad \text{so that} \quad u_{12} = a_{12}/\ell_{11}$$

$$a_{13} = \ell_{11}u_{13} \quad \text{so that} \quad u_{13} = a_{13}/\ell_{11}$$

and so on which defines row 2 of U.   This procedure is followed through column 2 of L, row 2 of U and so on until the factorization is complete.

In general, considering column k of the array A,

$$a_{jk} = \sum_{i=1}^{n} \ell_{ji} u_{ik}$$

but $u_{ik} = 0$ for $i > k$ and $u_{kk} = 1$, so that

$$a_{jk} = \sum_{i=1}^{k-1} \ell_{ji} u_{ik} + \ell_{jk}$$

from which

$$\ell_{jk} = a_{jk} - \sum_{i=1}^{k-1} \ell_{ji} u_{ik} \tag{1}$$

which is only necessary for each j from k to n since $\ell_{jk} = 0$ for $k > j$.

Similarly for row k of the array A,

$$a_{kj} = \sum_{i=1}^{n} \ell_{ki} u_{ij}$$

but $\ell_{ki} = 0$ for $i > k$ so that

$$a_{kj} = \sum_{i=1}^{k-1} \ell_{ki} u_{ij} + \ell_{kk} u_{kj}$$

from which

$$u_{kj} = \frac{a_{kj} - \sum_{i=1}^{k-1} \ell_{ki} u_{ij}}{\ell_{kk}} \qquad (2)$$

and since $u_{kj} = 0$ when $k > j$ and $u_{kk} = 1$, this is only necessary for each j from $k + 1$ to n.

The entire algorithm for triangular factorization is therefore:

  (i)   Column 1 of L is the same as column 1 of A

  (ii)   Row 1 of U is $u_{1j} = a_{1j}/\ell_{11}$

  (iii) For each k from 2 to n

         (a) find column k of L using equation (1) for j from k to n
         (b) find row k of U using equation (2) for j from k + 1 to n
             except when k = n

  (iv)   Row n of U contains only $u_{nn} = 1$

Write a program to perform the Crout reduction to triangular factors of the array

$$\begin{bmatrix} 10 & -7 & 3 & 5 \\ -6 & 8 & -1 & -4 \\ 3 & 1 & 4 & 11 \\ 5 & -9 & -2 & 4 \end{bmatrix}$$

Note that real arrays should be used, and L is not the name of a real array. Do not use subroutines.

Answer:

$$\begin{pmatrix} 10 & 0 & 0 & 0 \\ -6 & 3.8 & 0 & 0 \\ 3 & 3.1 & 2.447 & 0 \\ 5 & -5.5 & -2.342 & 9.925 \end{pmatrix}\begin{pmatrix} 1 & -0.7 & 0.3 & 0.5 \\ 0 & 1 & 0.211 & -0.263 \\ 0 & 0 & 1 & 4.215 \\ 0 & 0 & 0 & 1 \end{pmatrix}$$

PROBLEM 5.7: The algorithm outlined above can operate with the space shared for A, L and U as long as things are done in the appropriate order and if the diagonal of U is not stored (it can be assumed). EQUIVALENCE the three arrays A, L and U to make it work. Do not use subroutines.

PROBLEM 5.8: Triangular factorization can be used to solve linear equations. Suppose the equation is

$$Ax = y$$

If L and U are the triangular factors of A and the equation

$$Lz = y$$

is solved, and then the result z used to find

$$Ux = z$$

then one has found

$$L(Ux) = y$$

i.e.

$$Ax = y$$

Therefore the equations can be solved by:

(i) finding L and U as above

(ii) solving $Lz = y$ (by forward substitution)

(iii) solving $Ux = z$ (by back substitution)

The details are as follows:

(i) Forward substitution for $Lz = y$

$$y_j = \sum_{i=1}^{n} \ell_{ji} \, z_i$$

but $\ell_{ji} = 0$ for $i > j$, so that

$$y_j = \sum_{i=1}^{j} \ell_{ji} \, z_i = \sum_{i=1}^{j-1} \ell_{ji} \, z_i + \ell_{jj} \, z_j$$

from which

$$z_j = \frac{y_j - \sum_{i=1}^{j-1} \ell_{ji} \, z_i}{\ell_{jj}}$$

for j from 1 to n, but note that there is no sum for j = 1.

(ii)   Back substitution for Ux = z

$$z_j = \sum_{i=1}^{n} u_{ji} \, x_i$$

but $u_{ji} = 0$ for $j > i$ and $u_{jj} = 1$, so that

$$z_j = \sum_{i=j+1}^{n} u_{ji} \, x_i + x_j$$

from which

$$x_j = z_j - \sum_{i=j+1}^{n} u_{ji} \, x_i$$

for j = n, n-1, ..., but note that there is no sum for j = n.
Still with L and U EQUIVALENCED, solve by this means the equations

$$10x_1 - 7x_2 + 3x_3 + 5x_4 = 6$$
$$-6x_1 + 8x_2 - x_3 - 4x_4 = 5$$
$$3x_1 + x_2 + 4x_3 + 11x_4 = 2$$
$$5x_1 - 9x_2 - 2x_3 + 4x_4 = 7$$

It will be found that x, y, and z can also be EQUIVALENCED.   Do not use subroutines.

(Answer 5,4,-7,1)

6 The Use of Arrays in Subprograms

It is of course desirable that subprograms should be able to
handle array variables as arguments in the normal way. The complication is that the subroutine must know the layout of each array, and
this means that the dimensions of the array must be known by the
subroutine. The whole point of having subroutines is to allow people
to make their algorithms general so that they and others can use the
same subroutines in different programs. As far as arrays are
concerned, this means that a well-written subroutine is independent
of the actual size of arrays. The full specification of FORTRAN IV
allows for variable array dimensions to be used in subprograms, and
this is a great convenience. Unfortunately not all compilers support
this feature and for these computers it is not possible to make
subroutines general without violating some rules. First the happy
situation will be considered.

Suppose a main program defines a 5 x 5 real array called ARAY, and
a subroutine UNIT is to be used to define it as a unit matrix. This
subroutine should be able to create a unit matrix in any square array.
The dimensioning problem is taken care of as follows:

```
      DIMENSION ARAY(5,5)        main program
      CALL UNIT(ARAY,5)
          .
          .
          .
      END
      SUBROUTINE UNIT(U,N)       subroutine
      DIMENSION U(N,N)
      DO 35 K=1,N
      DO 36 L=1,N
   36 U(K,L)=0.0
   35 U(K,K)=1.0
      RETURN
      END
```

In the subroutine UNIT the array is called U, and the dimensions of
U are given using the variable N. U and N are subroutine dummy
arguments, and in this example when the subroutine is called by the
main program, the array ARAY is used wherever U appears in the subroutine. The call gives a value to the array size N which is
referred to whenever subscripts of U are used. Using a variable
dimension in this way is of great conveneince in array manipulation.

Any arrays that are used by a subroutine must be given in a DIMENSION statement in the subroutine itself. These could be either of fixed or variable dimension. However an array of variable dimension must be an argument of the subroutine, and so must the variable used for dimensioning.

EXAMPLE: Subroutine SUBY contains three arrays as follows:

(i)   Array ARGY is an argument of the subroutine call and has variable dimensions M x N.

(ii)   Array BARGY is an argument of the subroutine, but its size is always 71 and so a variable subscript has not been used.

(iii) Array PORKY is not an argument of the subroutine; it originates in the subroutine and by necessity is given a fixed dimension.

(iv)   The variable SP is a scalar as far as the subroutine is concerned. Any attempt to use it with a subscript in the subroutine would be an error.

```
SUBROUTINE SUBY(SP,ARGY,BARGY,M,N)
DIMENSION ARGY(M,N),BARGY(71),PORKY(1Ø,1Ø)
    .
    .
    .
RETURN
END
```

Every array in a program must originate somewhere with a fixed dimension. In the above example PORKY originates within subroutine SUBY, whereas ARGY and BARGY originate elsewhere. BARGY must have originated with length 71, but ARGY could have been any size. It must, however, appear in a DIMENSION statement with fixed subscripts presumably in the program that calls SUBY. The values of M and N should correspond to that fixed size. So variable dimensions are not a means of changing the size of an array - that is always fixed in FORTRAN - but they do provide a convenient way of communicating what that size is.

EXAMPLE: Here is a program to transpose the M x M matrix A. The transpose T of a square matrix A is such that

$$t_{ij} = a_{ji}$$

i.e.

$$\begin{pmatrix} 1 & 4 & 7 \\ 2 & 5 & 8 \\ 3 & 6 & 9 \end{pmatrix}$$

is the transpose of

$$\begin{pmatrix} 1 & 2 & 3 \\ 4 & 5 & 6 \\ 7 & 8 & 9 \end{pmatrix}$$

```
      SUBROUTINE TRANSP(A,M)
C    A SUBPROGRAM TO TRANSPOSE A
      DIMENSION A(M,M)
      DO 10 I=2,M
      JTOP=I-1
      DO 10 J=1,JTOP
      SAVE=A(I,J)
      A(I,J)=A(J,I)
      A(J,I)=SAVE
   10 CONTINUE
      RETURN
      END
```

Note the use of the variable SAVE.

The same arrangements apply to FUNCTION subprograms. Arrays can be communicated through any complicated subprogram network, but each array must originate somewhere with a fixed dimension. The variable subscript can be continued down through several levels of subprogram by continuing the array and its variable dimension as arguments. Some of the uses are illustrated in Fig. 5.13. The various uses of variables in the CALL statement should be noted; in particular an array name used with a subscript can be turned into a scalar as in the subprogram S3.

EXAMPLE: The FUNCTION subprogram listed below finds the element of array A which has the largest magnitude, and returns this absolute value.

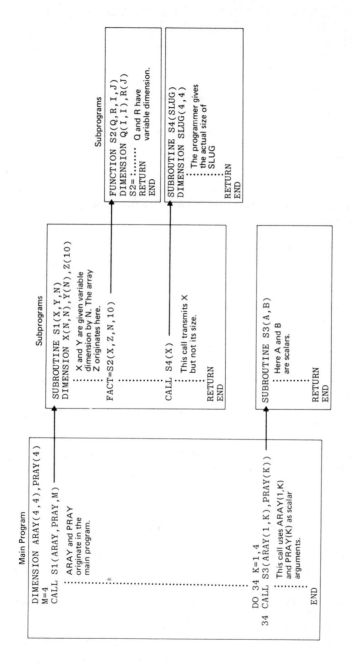

Fig. 5.13. Subprogram arrangement showing various uses of arrays as arguments.

```
      FUNCTION BIGEST(A,M,N)
C A FUNCTION TO RETURN LARGEST ABSOLUTE
C VALUE FROM THE M X N ARRAY A
      DIMENSION A(M,N)
      BIG=Ø.Ø
      DO 1Ø K=1,M
      DO 1Ø L=1,N
      IF(ABS(A(K,L)).GT.BIG)BIG=ABS(A(K,L))
 1Ø CONTINUE
      BIGEST=BIG
      RETURN
      END
```

PROBLEM 5.9:   (i) Write a subroutine TRIANG (A,N) for triangular factorization of the N x N array A without using additional arrays. (See Problems 5.6 and 5.7.)

(ii) Write a subroutine FORSUB(A,Y,N) to solve

$$Lz = y$$

by forward substitution, where the array A has been factored to contain L.   (See Problem 5.8.)

(iii) Write a subroutine BAKSUB(A,Y,N) to solve

$$Ux = z$$

where the array A has been factored to contain U, and the array z is already contained in Y.   (See Problem 5.8.)

(iv) Write a subroutine SOLVE(A,Y,N) which, using subroutines TRIANG, FORSUB, and BAKSUB solves

$$Ax = y$$

Can you make it put A back together again?

Unfortunately, some restricted versions of FORTRAN IV do not allow the variable dimension. The programmer in such a situation is faced with the awkward choice of using the same fixed subscripts everywhere and losing generality, or of violating in some way the strict rules of FORTRAN. The latter is the usual choice. In the previous section the arrangement of arrays in storage was described and knowledge of this allows the use of subscripting methods for subroutines which are, strictly speaking, illegal but allowed by most compilers. These are briefly described here.

For an array of one dimension there is no problem. Although the rules ask that the dimension be correct, in practice any dimension can be given in a subroutine and the subscripting will work:

```
      SUBROUTINE LIAR(LIES,N)
      DIMENSION LIES(1)
      DO 13 K=1,N
   13 LIES(K)=K
      RETURN
      END
```

The size of the array is transmitted but not used in the DIMENSION statement. The array is instead given the false dimension 1. This program will quite happily work just as if it did allow the variable subscript N, and so define LIES(K) = K from 1 to N.

With two dimensions the situation is more complex. The subroutine must take account of the actual dimensions in order to calculate the subscripts. The trick here is to pretend in the subroutine that the array has only one dimension and work with the equivalent one dimensional subscript. Therefore the earlier example which defined an N x N unit matrix in subroutine UNIT could be:

```
      SUBROUTINE UNIT(U,N)
C SUBROUTINE TO DEFINE N X N MATRIX U
      DIMENSION U(1)
      DO 35 K=1,N
      DO 36 L=1,N
C  36 U(K,L)=0.
      KL=K+(L-1)*N
   36 U(KL)=0.
C  35 U(K,K)=1.
      KK=K+(K-1)*N
   35 U(KK)=1
      RETURN
      END
```

Here the equivalent subscripts are worked out for the pretend one-dimensional array U. To help in understanding the operations, the equivalent statement in two dimensions is included by giving it as a comment and the variables used in subscripting are given names which resemble the equivalent, i.e. (KL) stand for (K,L). The subroutine, by the way, could be made much more efficient.

For an L x M array the equivalent of subscript (I,J) in one dimension is I + (J-1)*L.

For an L x M x N array, the equivalent of subscript (I,J,K) in one
dimension is I + (J-1)*L+(K-1)*L*M.

7 The COMMON Area

Much of the flexibility of FORTRAN depends on the use of dummy
arguments in functions and subroutines. Sometimes, however, a
programmer might prefer not to use long lists of subroutine arguments
but would wish instead to have an area in memory where space is
shared by program and subprograms. The COMMON statement allows this
to be done. Additionally "labelled" common areas can be defined in
which space is shared by variables only in specified subprograms.
The COMMON area is created in the main program by the COMMON
statement:

>   COMMON *variables*

and an ordered area of memory is reserved for the named variables.
The COMMON statement can be used in addition to, or instead of, a
DIMENSION statement, as illustrated:

>   DIMENSION A(5,5)   or   COMMON X,Y,Z,A(5,5)
>   COMMON X,Y,Z,A,

These forms are equivalent and cause space to be set aside for the
scalar variable X, Y and Z and the array A, a total of 28 locations.
It would be incorrect however to give the dimensions of A twice. An
EQUIVALENCE statement could follow which made the COMMON area longer,
for example

>   DIMENSION MORE(33)
>   COMMON I,J,IRAY(20)
>   EQUIVALENCE J,MORE

which defines an area 35 spaces long as shown in Fig. 5.14. It is
important to realise that the COMMON statement dictates the order of
variables in the COMMON area and that successive COMMON statements
add to the same area. One could not EQUIVALENCE I to J in the above
example.

It is also illegal to extend the common area backwards as the
statement

>   EQUIVALENCE I,MORE(3)

would attempt to do.

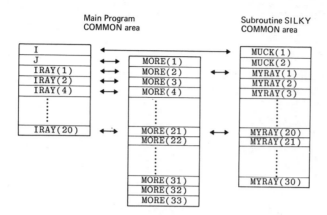

Fig. 5.14. Illustrating the correspondence between variables using COMMON and EQUIVALENCE statements.

Once a common area is created by a main program, subroutines or functions can make use of it if they have their own COMMON statements. In a subprogram the COMMON statement tells where in COMMON variables are to be found. In the process their names and even their type can be changed but in a one-to-one correspondence with the space allocated in the main program. The only restriction is that the subroutine should not try to define a COMMON area larger than the total space set aside in the main program. It can be smaller.

So in a subroutine the same COMMON area as defined above could be referred to as

```
SUBROUTINE SILKY
COMMON MUCK(2),MYRAY(3Ø)
```

which specifies the locations of two integer arrays. The array MYRAY is in effect equivalent to parts of MORE and IRAY as shown in Fig. 5.14.

EXAMPLE: The subroutine to create a unit matrix could operate in COMMON:

```
      DIMENSION ARAY(5,5)      main program
      COMMON ARAY
      CALL UNIT
        :
        :
      END

      SUBROUTINE UNIT          subroutine
      COMMON UNIT(5,5)
      DO 35 K=1,5
      DO 36 L=1,5
   36 U(K,L)=0.0
   35 U(K,K)=1.0
      RETURN
      END
```

Here, some generality has been lost - there is no way of making an area in COMMON variable in length. In fact a variable may not be mentioned in COMMON and be in the SUBROUTINE statement as a dummy argument at the same time. It may be in either, but not both.

A labelled COMMON area is also allowed, which need not be defined in the main program, only in those program modules which require it. Labelled COMMON areas must always be of the same length. The label is specified between slashes in the COMMON statement; in fact labelled and unlabelled entries can be intermixed in the same statement but this is confusing and therefore is poor style. The label of a common area may not be the same as any subprogram name (and this includes the library routines such as ATAN).

EXAMPLE: A main program calls two subroutines, SETUP and CRANK which share a matrix QUITE with each other through labelled common TURN but not with the main program. However the main program shares some variables with both programs through unlabelled common.

```
      COMMON A(3,3), Y(3), STEP       main program
        :
        :
      CALL SETUP
        :
        :
      CALL CRANK(DRIVE)
        :
        :
      END
```

```
SUBROUTINE SETUP                  subroutine
COMMON/TURN/SET(3,3)
COMMON A(3,3),STUFF(3),H
    .
    .
    .
RETURN
END

SUBROUTINE CRANK(DRIVE)          subroutine
COMMON/TURN/QUITE(3,3)
COMMON RUSH(9),Y(3),H
    .
    .
    .
RETURN
END
```

The storage arrangements known by these programs is shown in Fig. 5.15.

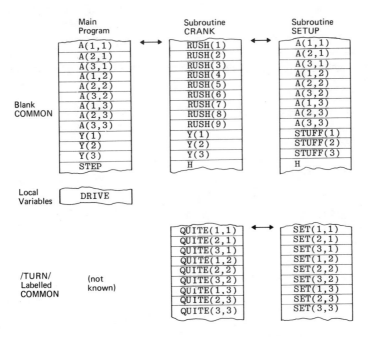

Fig. 5.15. Illustrating a storage arrangement
involving blank and labelled COMMON.

The COMMON areas in the subroutines could be defined in one statement, i.e. by

```
COMMON A(3,3),STUFF(3),H/TURN/SET(5,5)
```

in SETUP and by

```
COMMON/TURN/QUITE(5,5)//RUSH(9),Y(3),H
```

in CRANK. Note the use of two slashes in sequence to return to
blank common from labelled common.

   One disadvantage of COMMON is that normal DATA statements may never
refer to it. Data may never be entered during compilation to blank
COMMON. However a labelled COMMON block can have initial values
assigned by a BLOCK DATA subprogram. A BLOCK DATA subprogram begins
with the BLOCK DATA statement, and ends with an END statement. It
contains no executable statements. In the BLOCK DATA subprogram are
the labelled COMMON statements, DIMENSION or type statements if necessary, and DATA statements referring to variables in the labelled
COMMON area. Several labelled COMMON blocks can be referred to.
More than one BLOCK DATA subprogram is allowed, but if all or part
of an area is redefined then the last reference to it in a BLOCK
data subprogram is used for the initial value. The sole purpose of
the BLOCK DATA subprogram is to assign values to variables in labelled
COMMON.

EXAMPLE: The array NUMBRS in COMMON area COUNT is to be defined.
   Other variables in the same labelled COMMON are not initialized.
   The entire subprogram is

```
BLOCK DATA
DIMENSION A(4),B(4),NUMBRS(10),ARAY(5,5)
COMMON/COUNT/A,B,C,I,J,K,NUMBRS,ARAY
DATA NUMBRS/1,2,3,4,5,6,7,8,9,0/
END
```

8 Declarations of Type—REAL and INTEGER

   Up to this point it has always been assumed that the type (real or
integer) of a variable can only be given implicitly by the spelling
of its name: I,J,K,L,M or N to begin integers and anything else for
reals. In fact the type of a variable can be stated in a REAL or
INTEGER statement, which can also state the dimension of the variable.
Bearing in mind that the size should only be given once, the REAL,
INTEGER, DIMENSION and COMMON statements can be combined in many
ways.

EXAMPLE: The statements

```
     REAL XPART(21),YPART(21)
     INTEGER IPROD(1Ø),LUNG(15)
```

contain no surprises and are exactly equivalent to the single statement

```
     DIMENSION XPART(21),YPART(21),IPROD(1Ø),LUNG(15)
```

The statements

```
     REAL KWOTA(8),QUOTA(8)
     INTEGER YES(1Ø),NO(1Ø)
```

not only state the dimension of four arrays but also forces two changes of type. KWOTA becomes a real array and YES an integer one. This could not be accomplished by a single statement, but equivalent statements are

```
     REAL KWOTA
     INTEGER YES
     DIMENSION KWOTA(8),QUOTA(8),YES(1Ø),NO(1Ø)
```

These could be forced to share space in various ways by an EQUIVALENCE statement, such as

```
     EQUIVALENCE (KWOTA,QUOTA,YES,NO)
```

which compresses all the arrays into a single area, 10 locations long.

COMMON can also be involved. The following example produces a complicated layout as illustrated in Fig. 5.16. It would actually be bad style to create such an unnecessaily involved arrangement.

```
     REAL JOHN,LINDA,MARY,IMPULS,FRED(7)
     INTEGER IMPLIC(1ØØ),REFER,DAVID,OUTPUT,INFER(1Ø)
     DIMENSION MARY(8),REFER(8),EXPLIC(64),HERE(5)
     COMMON XAVIER,INPUT,MARY,INFER,IMPULS(15),IMPLIC
     EQUIVALENCE (JOHN,INPUT),(XAVIER,OUTPUT),(LINDA,MARY)
     EQUIVALENCE (INFER,REFER),(IMPLIC(37),EXPLIC),(DAVID,HERI
```

The type statements REAL and INTEGER can be used freely in subroutines with or without variable dimensions just as in the DIMENSION statement. It must be recalled, however, that the parameters of a CALL statement and the dummy arguments of the subroutine must correspond in type. A subroutine always assumes

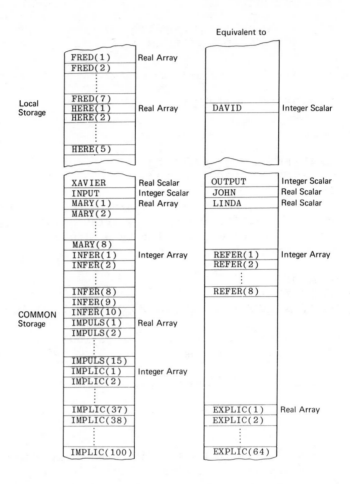

Fig. 5.16. Storage arrangement arising from a combination of
type, DIMENSION, COMMON, and EQUIVALENCE statements.

that its dummy arguments are of the type implied by their spelling
regardless of what may have been done elsewhere in the main program
or another subroutine. To change this an explicit declaration is
required in the subroutine itself. As before, variable dimensions
may not be used with variables in COMMON.

The ability to change type extends to both kinds of functions as
well. Suppose an arithmetic statement function which is real is

to be created which converts any angle in degrees to an equivalent in the range 0 - 360°. For reasons of his own the programmer wants to call this function MINE. To make this possible the program need only contain the statements

```
REAL MINE
MINE(THETA)=AMOD(THETA,360.)
```

which define the arithmetic statement function MINE to be a real function of a single argument.

The type of a function subprogram can also be controlled. One widely-used computer system contains a built-in function called SHIFT, which is an integer function of a single integer argument. Programmers get into trouble by not realizing that they must declare its type in a statement,

```
INTEGER SHIFT
```

before it can be expected to work properly. The declaration must be made separately in every program or subprogram that uses SHIFT. A programmer could create his own integer function shift using an INTEGER FUNCTION statement, which declares the type of the function explicitly.

```
  INTEGER FUNCTION SHIFT(I,ISHF)
  IF(ISHF)2,1,1
1 SHIFT=I*2**ISHF
  GO TO 3
2 SHIFT=(I-1)/2**(-ISHF))
3 RETURN
  END
```

This function does an arithmetic binary shift of the integer argument I by ISHF positions to the left (if the computer uses twos complement arithmetic). There is, of course, a REAL FUNCTION statement which gives an explicit declaration of the type of a real function subprogram.

9 Recommended Order of Statements

The order-dependence of certain statements of FORTRAN has been mentioned several times. All the fundamental information has now been assembled to allow this order to be spelled out. Many FORTRAN systems allow a relaxation of the order specified here, but it is wise to follow it in order to make programs as universal as possible.

In a main program the following statements should appear in the following order at the beginning before any other statements.

DIMENSION or type (REAL,INTEGER,COMPLEX,DOUBLE
                    PRECISION.LOGICAL, or EXTERNAL)
COMMON
EQUIVALENCE
DATA
Arithmetic statement function definitions

In a subprogram, the order should be

SUBROUTINE or FUNCTION (or REAL FUNCTION
                          or INTEGER FUNCTION)
DIMENSION or type (REAL,INTEGER,COMPLEX,DOUBLE
                    PRECISION,LOGICAL, or EXTERNAL)
COMMON
EQUIVALENCE
DATA
Arithmetic statement function definitions

In both cases the DIMENSION and type statements can be mixed among themselves.

10 Supplementary Problems

PROBLEM 5.10: Any linear ordinary differential equation can be expressed in matrix form by defining a number of additional variables. The equation

$$\frac{d^2y}{dt^2} + 2\,\frac{dy}{dt} + 5y = 1$$

could be written in terms of new variables y_1 and y_2 to be

$$\frac{dy_1}{dt} = y_2 \qquad\qquad (1)$$

and

$$\frac{dy_2}{dt} = \frac{d^2y_1}{dt^2} = -\,5y_1 - 2y_2 + 1 \qquad\qquad (2)$$

i.e. y_1 is the same as y and y_2 is dy/dt. The single second-order equation is now described by two first order equations which could be written in matrix form

$$\begin{bmatrix} \dfrac{dy_1}{dt} \\[2ex] \dfrac{dy_2}{dt} \end{bmatrix} = \begin{bmatrix} 0 & 1 \\ -5 & -2 \end{bmatrix} \begin{bmatrix} y_1 \\ y_2 \end{bmatrix} + \begin{bmatrix} 0 \\ 1 \end{bmatrix}$$

or

$$\frac{dy}{dt} = Ay + u$$

Where A is a matrix and y and u are vectors.

In the Runge-Kutta procedure (Problem 4.9) given

$$y(t_0) = y_0$$

it is possible to solve for $y(t_0 + h)$ by finding, in order

$$k_0 = h \left\{ Ay_0 + u \right\}$$

$$k_1 = h \left\{ A(y_0 + k_0/2) + u \right\}$$

$$k_2 = h \left\{ A(y_0 + k_0/2) + u \right\}$$

$$k_3 = h \left\{ A(y_0 + k_0) + u \right\}$$

and then finding the solution

$$y(t_0 + h) = \frac{1}{6} \left\{ k_0 + 2k_1 + 2k_2 + k_3 \right\} + y_0$$

This is the same procedure as before except that y, k_0, k_1, k_2 and k_3 are now vectors and the differential equation is in matrix form.

Write a subroutine to solve a system of nth order in this way. Using it obtain ten seconds of the response of

$$\frac{d^3y}{dt^3} + 3 \frac{d^2y}{dt^2} + 2 \frac{dy}{dt} = 0$$

for $y(0) = -1$, $\dot{y}(0) = -1$ and $\ddot{y}(0) = -1$. Try different values of step size; the solution will be wildly unstable if too large a step is chosen.

PROBLEM 5.11: Solve the Laplace equation

$$\frac{\partial^2 u}{\partial x^2} + \frac{\partial^2 u}{\partial y^2} = 0$$

for the electrostatic potential in a plane with a dipolar source
and zero potential at the edge, as in Fig. 5.17.   Scale and
truncate the answer to integers.   Print out as an array and draw
in isopotential lines by hand.   Investigate the convergence and
stability of the solution if over-relaxation is applied based on
similar principles to those described in Problem 5.2.

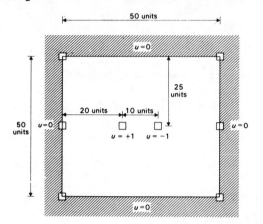

Fig. 5.17. An approximation to a dipolar source of potential.

The solution is found by devising a discrete model of the equation
and iterating to find the solution.   This is similar to what was
done in Problem 5.2.

Suppose this plane is divided into an array 51 cells by 51 cells,
and the potential at the centre of each cell is to be calculated.
If a potential $u_{k\ell}$ is considered, as in Fig. 5.18, the Laplace

$$u_{k-1,\ell}$$

$$u_{k,\ell-1} \qquad u_{k,\ell} \qquad u_{k,\ell+1}$$

$$u_{k+1,\ell}$$

Fig. 5.18. Adjacent cells in the plane.

equation can be modelled by using

$$\frac{\partial^2 u_{k\ell}}{\partial x^2} = (u_{k\ \ell+1} - u_{k\ \ell}) - (u_{k\ \ell} - u_{k\ \ell-1})$$

$$= u_{k\ \ell+1} - 2u_{k\ \ell} + u_{k\ \ell-1}$$

and

$$\frac{\partial^2 u_{k\ell}}{\partial y^2} = (u_{k+1\ \ell} - u_{k\ \ell}) - (u_{k\ \ell} - u_{k-1\ \ell})$$

$$= u_{k+1\ \ell} - 2u_{k\ \ell} + u_{k-1\ \ell}$$

so that a model for the Laplace equation is

$$u_{k\ \ell+1} + u_{k\ \ell-1} + u_{k+1\ \ell} + u_{k-1\ \ell} - 4u_{k\ \ell} = 0$$

from which

$$u_{k\ \ell} = \frac{u_{k\ \ell+1} + u_{k\ \ell-1} + u_{k+1\ \ell} + u_{k-1\ \ell}}{4}$$

Now the iterative solution of the equation can be done by calculating $u_{k\ell}$ throughout the whole array and then calculating again over and over until the solution changes very little between calculations. This is very straightforward except that the sources and the points next to the boundaries must be treated as special cases in order not to change their values. This kind of problem can consume large amounts of computer time. Make full use of the symmetries in the plane and do not attempt to achieve the final answer until hand checking of successive values suggests that the program appears to be working perfectly.

PROBLEM 5.12: The inverse of a matrix can be found by triangular factorization (Problems 5.6, 5.7, 5.8, 5.9). If the factored matrix is the N x N matrix

$$A = LU$$

then it is easily shown that

$$A^{-1} = U^{-1} L^{-1}$$

So to invert a matrix A the following steps have to be followed:

   (i)   Factor A into L and U (Problem 5.6)
  (ii)   Invert U to give $P = U^{-1}$
 (iii)   Invert L to give $Q = L^{-1}$
  (iv)   Form the product $PQ = U^{-1}L^{-1} = A^{-1}$

As it turns out, all these steps can be done in one array, i.e. not only can A be factored on top of itself, but also L and U can be inverted in their own space and the product can be formed without an additional array. The details follow:

(ii)   Inversion of U to give $P = U^{-1}$. It is easily shown that P is also upper triangular, and if the diagonal of U contains ones, so does that of P and they can be assumed rather than actually stored.

Now   PU = I (the unit matrix)

so that for $k = N, N-1, \ldots, 2$

$$\sum_{i=1}^{N} u_{ji} P_{ik} = I_{jk}$$

In the upper triangular part $k > j$, and $I_{jk} = 0$ so that

$$\sum_{i=1}^{N} u_{ji} P_{ik} = 0 \qquad \text{for } k > j$$

But $u_{ji} = 0$ for $j > i$ and $u_{jj} = 1$

$p_{ik} = 0$ for $i > k$ and $p_{kk} = 1$

Hence the sum only exists for $k > j$, so that

$$P_{jk} + \sum_{i=j+1}^{k-1} u_{ji} P_{ik} + u_{jk} = 0$$

and finally

$$P_{jk} = -u_{jk} - \sum_{i=j+1}^{k-1} u_{ji} P_{ik} \qquad (1)$$

So the recipe for inverting U is to use equation (1) over the range $k = N, N-1, \ldots, 2$ to find column k of P in the order $j = k-1, k-2, \ldots, 1$. When $k-1 < j+1$ (once each column) there is no sum.

(iii)   Inversion of L to give $Q = L^{-1}$. Q is also lower triangular, and

QL = I

so that for k = 1, 2, ... N-1

$$\sum_{i-1}^{N} \ell_{ji} \, q_{ik} = I_{jk}$$

But $\ell_{ji} = 0$ for $i > j$ and $q_{ik} = 0$ for $k > i$, so that the sum only exists for $j > k$. Therefore

$$\sum_{i=k}^{j} \ell_{ji} \, q_{ik} = I_{jk}$$

On the diagonal, $j = k$ and

$$q_{kk} = 1/\ell_{kk}$$

Off the diagonal, $j > k$ and

$$\sum_{i=k}^{j} \ell_{ji} \, q_{ik} = \sum_{i=k}^{j-1} \ell_{ji} \, q_{ik} + \ell_{jj} \, q_{jk} = 0$$

giving

$$q_{jk} = -\sum_{i=k}^{j-1} \frac{\ell_{ji} \, q_{ik}}{\ell_{jj}} \tag{2}$$

and leading directly to the recipe for inversion: For k from 1 to N-1 find

$$q_{kk} = 1/\ell_{kk}$$

and then use equation (2) to find column k of Q for j from k+1 to N. Finally find

$$q_{NN} = 1/\ell_{NN}$$

(iv) Multiplying P by Q. This is quite straightforward but if P and Q are stored in the same array the subscripting must be done carefully. Suppose the result is called R

$$R = PQ$$

$$r_{jk} = \sum_{i=1}^{N} p_{ji} \, q_{ik}$$

but $p_{ji} = 0$ for $j > i$

            $p_{jj} = 1$ (and may not be stored if all the arrays are
                    stored together)

and $q_{ik} = 0$ for $k > i$

Therefore

$$r_{jk} = q_{jk} + \sum_{i=j+1}^{N} p_{ji} q_{ik} \qquad (3)$$

if $j \geq k$ (but note there is no sum when $j = N$)

or

$$r_{jk} = \sum_{i=k}^{N} p_{ji} q_{ik} \qquad (4)$$

if $j < k$.

The procedure is thus for k from 1 to N to find r_{jk} using either
equation (3) or equation (4) for j from 1 to N-1. The last
element r_{Nk} is each row is the same as q_{Nk}.

Write separate subroutines to invert L, invert U, and multiply
the inverses together. A subroutine for triangular factorization
was prepared in Problem 5.9. Finally, write a subroutine which
calls on these and inverts an N x N matrix using this method.

6 Special Variable Types

1 Introduction

This course has stressed throughout the distinction between real
and integer variables and pointed out the circumstances in which
each should be used. In addition to these types, FORTRAN IV allows
others which can be used to meet special requirements. Logical
expressions have already been encountered as part of the logical IF
statement. It is possible to create logical variables which have
only the values .TRUE. or .FALSE., and these can be useful in
decision making and branching. There are also double precision
variables or constants which are used to obtain increased accuracy
or precision in calculations where the usual accuracy of the
computer is insufficient. Likewise, FORTRAN has special facilities
for convenient handling of complex numbers when defined as complex
variables or constants. These new types of variables can be used in
expressions, but the ways of using them among themselves and with
real and integer variables are strictly limited to certain allowed
combinations. For these new types of variables, special built-in
functions of various types with assorted types of arguments are
provided, as will be seen. Finally, the name of the program can be
made into an external variable and so transmitted through CALL
statements. This chapter describes the uses of these four special
variable types.

2 Logical Variables, Constants, and Expressions

Any variable can be defined as being of logical. type by the
LOGICAL statement:

     LOGICAL *variable names*

179

The specification that a particular variable is logical is a
complete one; the same variable cannot be real or integer or any
other type at the same time. Since there is no implicit spelling
of names for logical variables, they can only exist if there is a
LOGICAL statement to declare them. The LOGICAL statement is order-
dependent just like any other type statement (see Chapter 5,
Section 9).

Logical variables can be arrays, and so the dimension information
can be included in the LOGICAL statement, or in other ways as in
Chapter 5, Section 8.

EXAMPLES:

   (i)   The statement

        LOGICAL TRUTH,ANSWER(1Ø),INCLU

defines the variables TRUTH, ANSWER, and INCLU as being of type
logical. The logical variable ANSWER is an array of 10 logical
values. None of the named variables could appear in any other
type statement. However, the variables TRUTH and INCLU could
appear in DIMENSION or COMMON statements and so might be arrays
themselves.

   (ii)   The statements

        DIMENSION LOGS(16),VALUES(2Ø)
        LOGICAL LOGS

define a logical array LOGS of 16 logical values. The array
VALUES is evidently real.

   (iii)   The statements

        COMMON BEANS(6),DECIDE
        DIMENSION WHY(2),PEAS(4),NUTS(4),LUCY(4)
        LOGICAL DECIDE,WHY,WHERE(4),PARK
        EQUIVALENCE (BEANS,WHY),(PEAS,LUCY,WHERE)
        EQUIVALENCE (NUTS,PARK)

define the storage layout illustrated in Fig. 6.1.

There are two possible logical constants, .TRUE. and .FALSE. whose
values are self-explanatory. Logical variables and constants can
only be used in limited circumstances in a FORTRAN program.

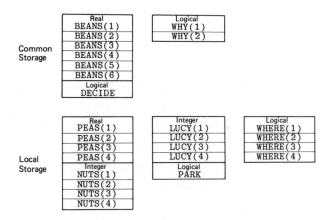

Fig. 6.1. A storage arrangement created by
COMMON, DIMENSION, LOGICAL, and EQUIVALENCE.

Together they can be combined into logical expressions using the
logical operations .AND., .OR., and .NOT. and with other variable
types by means of the relational operators .GT., .GE., .LT., .LE.,
.EQ., and .NE. These logical expressions are permitted only in the
logical IF statement or in arithmetic statements. Logical values
can also be assigned to logical variables in DATA statements and
logical variables can be used in READ and WRITE statements.

A logical expresison is something which is easily understood but
more difficult to define precisely. First consider any relational
expression:

> *arithmetic   relational   arithmetic*
> *expression   operator   expression*

Actually only certain combinations of *arithmetic expression* may be
used, as Fig. 6.2 indicates. Integer expressions may only be
compared to integer expressions. Real and double-precision
expressions may be compared to themselves and each other, whereas
complex and logical expressions may not be used with the relational
operators at all. Within these limitations relational expressions
can be formed which, when evaluated, have the logical values .TRUE.
and .FALSE.

	Real	Integer	Double precision	Complex	Logical
Real	YES		YES		
Integer		YES			
Double precision	YES		YES		
Complex					
Logical					

Arithmetic expression 1 — Relational operator — Arithmetic expression 2

Expression 2

Expression 1

Fig. 6.2. Allowed relational combinations of FORTRAN marked YES, others shaded. In effect only like types can be compared except that real and double precision can be mixed. Logical or complex expressions cannot be used at all.

A logical expression is then some combination of logical variables, logical constants, and valid relational combinations using the logical operators .NOT., .AND., and .OR., defined according to the truth table of Fig. 6.3.

Logical expression a — Logical operator — Logical expression b

Logical expression a	Operator	Logical expression b	Logical result
	·NOT·	·TRUE· ·FALSE·	·FALSE· ·TRUE·
·TRUE· ·TRUE· ·FALSE· ·FALSE·	·AND·	·TRUE· ·FALSE· ·TRUE· ·FALSE·	·TRUE· ·FALSE· ·FALSE· ·FALSE·
·TRUE· ·TRUE· ·FALSE· ·FALSE·	·OR·	·TRUE· ·FALSE· ·TRUE· ·FALSE·	·TRUE· ·TRUE· ·TRUE· ·FALSE·

Fig. 6.3. Truth table for the logical operations of FORTRAN.

The logical operator .NOT. must be followed by a logical expression, and the operators .AND. and .OR. must be both preceded and followed by logical expressions. Parentheses can be used in logical expressions to specify the order of computation. In the absence of parentheses the order is taken according to the hierarchy shown in Table 6.1.

( )	expressions in brackets	high priority
**	exponentiation	
* or /	multiplication or division	
+ or -	addition or subtraction	
.GT., .GE., .EQ., .LE., .LT., .NE.		
.NOT.		
.AND.		
.OR.		low priority

Table 6.1   The hierarchy of logical, relational and
arithmetic operations in FORTRAN IV

The logical expression, which has the result either .TRUE. or .FALSE., is used in either logical IF statements or an arithmetic statement, and nowhere else. The arithmetic assignment statement

logical variable = logical expression

causes the *logical expression* to be evaluated and the result, either .TRUE. or .FALSE. becomes the new value of the logical variable. No mode conversion is allowed - if the left-hand side is a logical variable, then the right-hand side can only be a logical expression.

EXAMPLES:

   (i)   JURY=.TRUE.

JURY must be a logical variable declared in a LOGICAL statement. The value .TRUE. is assigned to it.

   (ii)   SWITCH=A.GT.4.∅.OR.I.LT.73

SWITCH must be logical, A real, and I integer. SWITCH will be assigned value .FALSE. unless either A is greater than 4.0 or I is less than 73.

   (iii)   EOR=(A.AND.(.NOT.B)).OR.((.NOT.A).AND.B)

EOR, A, and B must be all of type logical. The exclusive OR of A and B is formed.

The logical IF statement was described in Chapter 3, and has the form

IF *(logical expression) executable statement*

This is the only other place where logical expressions may be used. When this statement is reached the *logical expression* is evaluated. If the result is .TRUE. then the *executable statement* is obeyed, otherwise the result is .FALSE. and the next FORTRAN statement in order is obeyed.

Logical variables can be defined in DATA statements to have initial values .TRUE. or .FALSE. as in the example:

```
LOGICAL QRAY(4),BEER
DATA QRAY/4*.TRUE./,BEER/.FALSE./
```

Alternatively the single letters .T. or .F. can be used:

```
LOGICAL TREE(3)
DATA TREE/.T.,.T.,.F./
```

If a logical variable is included in the list of a READ or WRITE statement, then the accompanying FORMAT statement must contain the appropriate logical field, designated by the L specification:

L*w*

where *w* is the width of the field of input or output in spaces. In a WRITE statement, the letter T for .TRUE. or F for .FALSE. would be printed right-justified in the field, for example in the following program which prints the exclusive OR of A and B:

```
      LOGICAL A,B,C
C DEFINE A AND B
      A=.TRUE.
      B=.FALSE.
C FORM EXCLUSIVE OR OF A AND B
      C=(A.AND.(.NOT.B)).OR.(B.AND.(.NOT.A))
C PRINT THE RESULT USING LOGICAL FORMAT
      WRITE(6,1Ø)A,B,C
   1Ø FORMAT(1X,3HA =,L2,4H B =,L2,1ØH A.EOR.B =,L2)
      STOP
      END
```

would print

A = T B = F A.EOR.B = T
. . . .

In response to a READ statement referring to fields of L format, the input should contain either T or F as the first nonblank character within the field.

INPUTS		OUTPUTS	
A	B	SUM	CARRY
F	F	F	F
F	T	T	F
T	F	T	F
T	T	F	T

Fig. 6.4. Truth table for logical half-addition.

PROBLEM 6.1: Binary half-addition obeys the truth table shown in Fig. 6.4, so that if A and B are the inputs and SUM and CARRY the outputs,

$$SUM = A.\bar{B} + B.\bar{A} \quad (A \text{ and not } B \text{ or } B \text{ and not } A)$$

$$CARRY = A.B \quad (A \text{ and } B)$$

Write a program to simulate half-addition.

SOLUTION: Fig. 6.5 shows the flow diagram of the solution listed below. Note that a function is used for the exclusive OR operation. It is made to be of type logical by declaring its name in the LOGICAL statement.

```
      LOGICAL A,B,SUM,CARRY,EOR
      EOR(A,B) = (A.AND.(.NOT.B)).OR.(B.AND.(.NOT.A))
C ASK FOR AND READ IN THE INPUTS
    5 WRITE(6,1Ø)
   1Ø FORMAT(1X,33HPROVIDE INPUTS A AND B FORMAT 2L3)
      READ(5,2Ø)A,B
   2Ø FORMAT(2L3)
C FORM THE SUM AND CARRY TERMS
      SUM=EOR(A,B)
      CARRY=A.AND.B
C PRINT THE RESULTS
      WRITE(6,3Ø)A,B
   3Ø FORMAT(1X,1ØHINPUTS A =,L2,4H B =,L2)
      WRITE(6,4Ø)SUM,CARRY
   4Ø FORMAT(1X,13HOUTPUTS SUM =,L2,8H CARRY =,L2)
      GO TO 5
      END
```

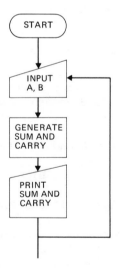

Fig. 6.5. Flow diagram for a program to do half-addition
using logical variables and expressions.

In this solution, an arithmetic statement function of type logical
has been used. It is also possible to create function subprograms

of type logical using the LOGICAL FUNCTION statement for example
for the NAND (not AND) operation:

```
      LOGICAL FUNCTION NAND(A,B)
C FUNCTION FOR THE NOT AND OF TWO LOGICAL ARGUMENTS
      LOGICAL A,B
      NAND=.NOT.(A.AND.B)
      RETURN
      END
```

Any program which used this function would have to include a
LOGICAL statement declaring the type of NAND:

```
      LOGICAL NAND,X,Y,Z
         .
         .
         .
      Z=NAND(NAND(X,NAND(X,Y)),NAND(Y,NAND(X,Y)))
         .
         .
         .
```

in which Z is again the exclusive OR of X and Y calculated· using
only the NAND function.

As a final word about logical variables, it should be said that they
are an infrequently used facility and in fact there is no need for
them in structuring a normal FORTRAN program which does numerical
calculations. As with many facilities in FORTRAN, a programmer can
create quite a bad program by over-indulgence in the use of logical
variables. Unless they aid program clarity or provide needed logical
facilities, they should not be used.

PROBLEM 6.2:   Fig. 6.6 illustrates a full binary adder with inputs
   A,B, and C (a carry input). Write a program to generate and print
   the sum and carry output using a function NOR(X,Y) defined as
   (.NOT.X.OR.Y) for all operations, i.e. once the NOR function has
   been defined, the FORTRAN operations .NOT., .AND., and .OR. should
   not be used. Referring to Fig. 6.6,

$$S = A + B + C_{IN} \quad \text{where } A + B = \text{exclusive OR of A and B}$$

$$C_{OUT} = (A + B).C_{IN} + A.B$$

Both these equations can be rewritten entirely in terms of the NOR
operation.

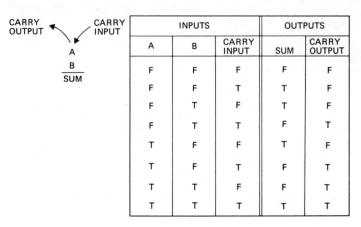

Fig. 6.6. Truth table for full binary addition.

3 Double Precision Variables, Constants, and Expressions

Any variable can be defined as being of double precision type by the DOUBLE PRECISION statement:

DOUBLE PRECISION *variable names*

The specification of double precision is a complete one; the same variable cannot be of any other type. Since there is no implicit spelling of names of double precision variables, they can only exist if there is a DOUBLE PRECISION statement to declare them. The DOUBLE PRECISION statement is order-dependent like any other type statement (see Chapter 5 Section 9).

Double precision variables can be arrays, and so the dimension information can be included in the DOUBLE PRECISION statement, or in other ways such as through COMMON or DIMENSION statements. In using COMMON or EQUIVALENCE statements with double precision variables there is a special complication because double precision variables take twice as much space as reals, integers, or logicals. This must be allowed for in laying out COMMON and using EQUIVALENCE.

EXAMPLE:

```
COMMON SLUG(1∅)
DIMENSION IRAY(5)
DOUBLE PRECISION PRECIS(4),DUBBL
EQUIVALENCE(SLUG,PRECIS),(IRAY,DUBBL)
```

This storage arrangement is illustrated in Fig. 6.7.

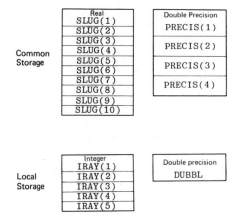

Fig. 6.7. Illustrating a storage arrangement using
COMMON, DIMENSION and DOUBLE PRECISION statements.
Each double precision variable takes twice the
space of reals, integers or logicals.

Constants of double precision are written in FORTRAN programs
using a notation similar to exponential form, with the letter D to
indicate double precision. In general these are written

real number D *integer exponent*

EXAMPLES:

1.∅D∅ means 1.0 with double precision accuracy, i.e. double the
usual number of zeroes
2.73D-36 means 2.73×10^{-36} with double precision accuracy

Double precision constants and variables can be used in arithmetic
expressions in FORTRAN in all the circumstances where real numbers
are allowed. In fact, ordinary reals and double precision numbers

can be mixed in arithmetic expressions although if this is done the ordinary real numbers will dominate the precision of the results. Therefore it is usually self-defeating to mix them. The operations of addition, subtraction, multiplication and division can be done between double precision numbers, or a mixture of real numbers and double precision in which case the double precision may be lost from the result. For exponentiation, a real number or a double precision number may be raised to a power which is real or double precision or integer. The allowed mixtures of operations for all variable types are summarized in Section 5 of this chapter.

In arithmetic statements, again any assignments are allowed for double precision as for reals, and mode conversions are performed. Therefore in a statement like

$$variable = expression$$

the *variable* might be real or integer or double precision. The *expression* could likewise be in real or integer or double precision, or even a mixture of real and double precision. After the *expression* is evaluated in its own mode, the result replaces the *variable* after mode conversion if necessary. Again, a mode conversion from double precision to real would probably result in a loss of precision. The allowed conversions between all variable types are summarized in Section 6.4.

In a DATA statement, double precision values can be assigned to double precision variables, as:

```
DOUBLE PRECISION X
DATA X/1.5D0/
```

For reading or writing double precision data in READ and WRITE statements, a double precision field specification is available, the D field:

D *w.d*

which is similar to E format. *w* is the total width of the field and *d* is the number of decimal digits expected in input or printed in output. As with the E field, spaces are required for signs, exponent and the letter D to be printed. Therefore for output *w* should be at least 7 greater than *d*.

EXAMPLE: This program obtains and prints the value of π to 30 significant digits. This assumes that double precision on the computer is 30 digits; it may actually be a lot less.

```
      DOUBLE PRECISION PIE
      PIE=4.ØDØ*DATAN(1.ØDØ)
      WRITE(6,2Ø)PIE
   2Ø FORMAT(1X,D4Ø.3Ø)
      STOP
      END
```

In the example, all the constants in the arithmetic statement have
been written carefully as double precision to ensure a double
precision result. The function DATAN is a special, built-in
double precision function for the arctangent. Because FORTRAN
already knows that DATAN is of type double precision, it has not
been necessary to declare it as such in the DOUBLE PRECISION
statement. Table 6.2 lists the double precision functions which
are part of standard FORTRAN.

Name	Meaning
DABS(D)	Absolute value of D. (Double)
DATAN(D)	Arctangent(D), angle in range $-\pi/2$ to $\pi/2$. (Double)
DATAN(D1,D2)	Arctangent(D1/D2) in range $-\pi$ to π. (Double)
DBLE(X)	Conversion real X to double precision. (Double)
DCOS(D)	Cosine of D, D in radians. (Double)
DEXP(D)	Exponential function e^D. (Double)
DLOG(D)	Natural logarithm, log D. (Double)
DLOG1Ø(D)	Logarithm base 10, $\log_{10}(D)$. (Double)
DMAX1(D1,D2,....)	Maximum of D1,D2,.... (Double)
DMIN1(D1,D2,....)	Minimum of D1,D2,.... (Double)
DMOD(D1,D2)	Remainder of D1/D2. (Double)
DSIGN(D1,D2)	Transfer sign; (sign D2)*DABS(D1). (Double)
DSIN(D)	Sine of D, D in radians. (Double)
DSQRT(D)	Square root of D, D positive. (Double)
IDINT(D)	Integer part of D. (Integer)
SNGL(D)	Truncate D to single precision. (Real)

Table 6.2. Built-in functions of FORTRAN for use with double precision.
All but IDINT and SNGL have results of double precision. All but DBLE
take double precision arguments, D, D1, or D2; X is a real argument
                    for DBLE.

As might be expected, it is possible to define double precision
arithmetic statement functions and function subprograms.

EXAMPLES:
  (i)   The following program contains the double precision arithmetic
statement function ANGL which converts its double precision argument
in degrees to a double precision result in radians. Note that the
function name, the name of its dummy argument and the names of the
variables used with it have all been declared to be double
precision.

```
      DOUBLE PRECISION ANGL,X,Y,Z
      ANGL(Z)=4.ØDØ*DATAN(1.ØDØ)*Z/18Ø.ØDØ
         .
         .
         .
      Y=ANGL(X)
         .
         .
         .
      END
```

(ii)   A double precision function is used in the following program
to evaluate the power series for sin(x) until the next term
contributes less than one part in 10^{25} to the sum. This assumes
double precision accuracy in the particular computer of at least
25 decimal digits; on some machines it could be a lot less. Note
that the function name and variables used with it are declared in
a DOUBLE PRECISION statement, and the careful use of double
precision quantities in the subprogram.

```
      DOUBLE PRECISION DSIN1,X,Y
    C ASK FOR AND INPUT THE ANGLE IN DEGREES
    1Ø WRITE(6,2Ø)
    2Ø FORMAT(1X,36HENTER ANGLE IN DEGREES FORMAT D2Ø.1Ø)
       READ(5,3Ø)X
    3Ø FORMAT(D2Ø.1Ø)
    C EVALUATE THE SINE
       Y=DSIN1(X)
    C PRINT THE RESULT
       WRITE(6,4Ø)X,Y
    4Ø FORMAT(6H SINE ,D2Ø.1Ø,11H DEGREES IS,D35.25)
       GO TO 1Ø
       END
```

The sum for sin(x) with x in radians is

$$\sin(x) = x - \frac{x^3}{3!} + \frac{x^5}{5!} - \frac{x^7}{7!} + \ldots$$

which has the recurrence relationship for the term of power n, t_n:

$$t_n = \frac{-x^2}{n(n-1)} t_{n-2} \quad \text{for } n = 3,5,7, \ldots$$

```
      DOUBLE PRECISION FUNCTION DSIN1(Z)
      DOUBLE PRECISION Z,Y,SUM,ANGL,XNUM,YSQ,A,TERM
      ANGL(A)=4.ØDØ*DATAN(1.ØDØ)*A/18Ø.ØDØ
C CONVERT TO RADIANS
      Y=ANGL(Z)
C INITIALIZE THE SUM
      SUM=Y
      YSQ=Y*Y
      TERM=Y
      XNUM=3.ØDØ
C PERFORM THE RECURRENCE
   1Ø TERM=-TERM*YSQ/XNUM/(XNUM-1.ØDØ)
      SUM=SUM+TERM
C TEST TO SEE IF EVALUATION IS FINISHED
      IF(DABS(TERM/SUM).LT.1.ØD-25)GO TO 2Ø
      XNUM=XNUM+2.ØDØ
      GO TO 1Ø
   2Ø DSIN1=SUM
      RETURN
      END
```

PROBLEM 6.3:   The Newton-Raphson iteration for finding roots of an equation

$$f(x) = 0$$

uses the recurrence

$$x_n = x_{n-1} - \frac{f(x_{n-1})}{f'(x_{n-1})}$$

where x_n is an improvement on the approximate root x_{n-1}.   If the function is very flat near the root, then $f(x)$ and $f'(x)$ will be small and there could be difficulty in evaluating $f(x)$ or $f'(x)$, and in calculating the new x_n using their ratio.   Double precision arithmetic can help in such a situation.

By solving for $g'(x) = 0$ using the Newton-Raphson iteration, locate the position and value of the minimum of $g(x)$ for

(i) $g(x) = x^4 - 5.2\ x^3 + 10.14\ x^2 - 8.788\ x + 4.5561$

(Answer 1.7 at x = 1.3)

(ii) $g(x) = x^8 - 13.6\ x^7 + 80.92\ x^6 - 275.128\ x^5 + 584.647\ x^4$

$- 795.11992\ x^3 + 675.851932\ x^2 - 328.2709384\ x$

$+ 71.0575441$

Compare the success or otherwise of the solution with and without judicious use of double precision. Because double precision arithmetic is slow, only use it where necessary.

4 Complex Variables, Constants, and Expressions

Complex quantities with real and imaginary components arise in many problems of engineering and science. Any variable can be defined as being complex by the COMPLEX statement:

COMPLEX *variable names*

That a variable is complex is a complete specification; it cannot be of any other type at the same time. Note particularly that a variable cannot be complex and double precision at the same time. Since there is no implicit spelling of names for complex variables, they only exist if they are declared in a COMPLEX statement. The COMPLEX statement is order-dependent like any other type statement (see Section 9 of Chapter 5).

A complex variable is, in effect, two real numbers one standing for the real part and the other for the imaginary part of a complex number. Complex variables can be arrays, and so the dimension information can be included in the COMPLEX statement, or in other ways such as through COMMON or DIMENSION statements. Because a complex variable is a pair of numbers, it occupies twice as much storage as do reals, integers or logicals. Therefore, just as with double precision variables but for different reasons, double space has to be allowed for complex variables in laying out COMMON and using EQUIVALENCE.

EXAMPLE:

```
      COMMON RESPON(5)
      DIMENSION IMPULS(8)
      DOUBLE PRECISION PRECIS(4)
      COMPLEX RESPON,RATIO
      EQUIVALENCE(RESPON,PRECIS),(IMPULS,RATIO)
```

This storage arrangement is illustrated in Fig. 6.8.

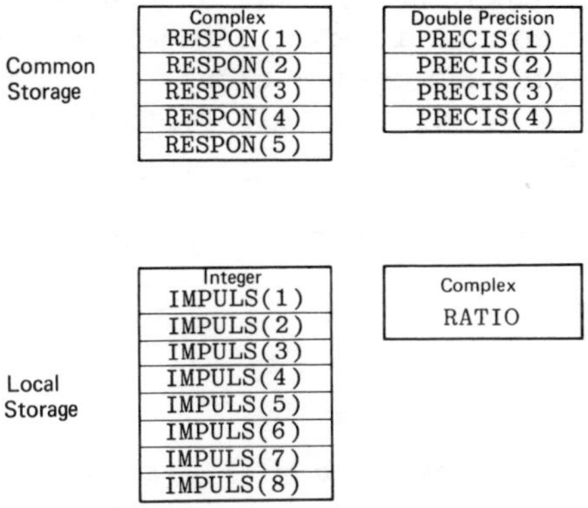

Fig. 6.8. Illustrating a storage arrangement using
COMMON, DIMENSION, DOUBLE PRECISION, and COMPLEX.
Each complex or double precision variable takes twice
the space of reals, integers or logicals.

Complex constants are written in FORTRAN programs as a pair of real numbers in parentheses (brackets) with a comma between.   The numbers may be signed;   the brackets are always required regardless of context.

EXAMPLES: $(1.\emptyset,1.\emptyset)$ is the complex number $1 + j1$
            $(\emptyset.\emptyset,1.414)$ is the complex number $j1.414$
            $(-2.\emptyset,+1.\emptyset)$ is the complex number $-2 + j1$

Complex constants and variables can be used in arithmetic expressions of FORTRAN in most but not all circumstances where reals are allowed, and real numbers and complex numbers can be mixed in arithmetic expressions.   The operations of addition, subtraction, multiplication, and division can be done between complex numbers and between a mixture of reals and complex numbers;   the results in both cases are complex.   As for exponentiation, a complex number may be raised only to an integer power.   The allowed mixtures for

all variable types are summarized in Section 5 of this Chapter.
Note particularly that complex and double precision can never be
mixed.

There are also restrictions in the ways which complex values can be
assigned in arithmetic statements. In the statement

$$variable = expression$$

if *variable* is complex, then the *expression* can be only real or
complex. Note that conversion from an integer is not allowed. If
variable is real, then the *expression* cannot be complex. The
allowed conversions between all variable types are summarized in
Section 5 of this Chapter.

In a DATA statement, complex values can be assigned to complex
variables, as:

```
COMPLEX OHMS
DATA OHMS/(1.Ø,1.Ø)/
```

For reading or writing a complex variable in READ or WRITE
statements, two real field specifications are used (either F or E
fields). The one-to-one correspondence between the READ or WRITE
list and the FORMAT *specification* is preserved by providing two
real fields for each complex variable.

EXAMPLE: The second order differential equation

$$\frac{d^2y}{dt^2} + 2\,\frac{dy}{dt} + y = x(t)$$

could describe the behaviour of a variety of systems, for example
either the mechanical or electrical systems of Fig. 6.9.   The
complex ratio

$$\frac{Y(\omega)}{X(\omega)} = \frac{1}{-\omega^2 + 2j\omega + 1}$$

is called the frequency response of the system because it describes
the relationship between input and output for sinusoidal excitation
at a frequency ω. The following program evaluates the frequency
response for a given   value of ω and prints it both as a complex
number and in polar form (magnitude and phase).

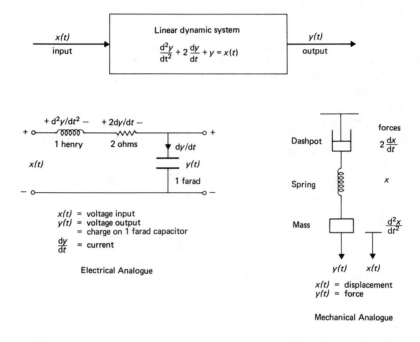

Fig. 6.9. A linear dynamic system and two physical interpretations of it. The frequency response is calculated as an example of complex arithmetic in FORTRAN.

```
      COMPLEX RESP,R
      ANGL(R)=ATAN2(AIMAG(R),REAL(R))
C ASK FOR AND ACCEPT THE FREQUENCY AS INPUT
   1Ø WRITE(6,2Ø)
   2Ø FORMAT(34H INPUT A FREQ IN RADIANS/SEC F1Ø.5)
      READ(5,3Ø)OMEGA
   3Ø FORMAT(F1Ø.5)
C WORK OUT RESPONSE AT FREQUENCY OMEGA
      RESP=1./CMPLX(-OMEGA*OMEGA+1.Ø,2.*OMEGA)
C ALSO OBTAIN MAGNITUDE AND PHASE
      XMAG=CABS(RESP)
      XPHA=ANGL(RESP)
C PRINT THE RESULTS
      WRITE(6,4Ø)OMEGA,RESP
   4Ø FORMAT(12H RESPONSE AT,F1Ø.5,15H RADIANS/SEC IS,
     1F1Ø.5,5H + J ,F1Ø.5)
      WRITE(6,5Ø)XMAG,XPHA
   5Ø FORMAT(1X,23HIN POLAR FORM MAGNITUDE,F1Ø.5,
     19H AT ANGLE,F1Ø.5,8H RADIANS)
      GO TO 1Ø
      END
```

In the example, the functions AIMAG, REAL, CMPLX and CABS are special
built-in functions of FORTRAN provided to deal with complex numbers.
Table 6.3 lists the complex functions and functions of complex arguments which are part of standard FORTRAN. The arithmetic statement
function ANGL used in the example is itself a real function of a
complex argument - hence it has not been named as complex but its
dummy argument has.

As might be expected, it is possible to define complex function subprograms and complex arithmetic statement functions; the following
simple example has both.

EXAMPLE: A complex function subprogram CARTES is used to convert complex
numbers given in polar form by the real variables XMAG (magnitude) and
XANG (phase in degrees) into a Cartesian complex number CMPLEX. The
subprogram contains a complex arithmetic statement function RECT and
a real arithmetic statement function ANGL.

Main program:

```
      COMPLEX CARTES,CMPLEX
        .
        .
        .
      CMPLEX=CARTES(XMAG,XANG)
        .
        .
        .
      END
```

Function subprogram:

```
          COMPLEX FUNCTION CARTES(X,Y)
          COMPLEX RECT
          RECT(P,Q)=CMPLX(P*COS(Q),P*SIN(Q))
          ANGL(Z)=4.0*ATAN(1.0)*Z/180.0
          CARTES=RECT(X,ANGL(Y))
          RETURN
          END
```

NAME	MEANING
AIMAG(C)	Extract imaginary part of C. (Real)
CABS(C)	Modulus of C; if C=C(XR,XI) then CABS(C)=SQRT(XR*XR+XI+XI). (Real)
CCOS(C)	Cosine of C; if C=C(XR,XI) radians then CCOS(C)=(Cos(XR)*Cosh(XI),-Sin(XR)*Sinh(XI)). (Complex)
CEXP(C)	Exponential e^C; if C=(XR,XI) then CEXP(C)=e^{XR}*(Cos(XI),Sin(XI)). (Complex)
CLOG(C)	Natural logarithm $\log_e C$; if C=(XR,XI) then CLOG(C)=(0.5*ALOG(CABS(C)),ATAN2(XI,XR)). (Complex)
CMPLX(XR,XI)	Convert two reals to complex (XR,XI). (Complex)
CONJ(C)	Complex conjugate of C; if C=(XR,XI) then CONJ(C)=(XR,-XI). (Complex)
CSIN(C)	Sine of C; if C=(XR,XI) then CSIN(C)=(Sin(XR)*Cosh(XI),Cos(XR)*Sinh(XI)). (Complex)
CSQRT(C)	Square root of C, if C=(XR,XI) and A=ATAN2(XI,XR) then CSQRT(C)=CABS(C)*(COS(A),SIN(A)). (Complex)
REAL(C)	Extract real part of C. (Real)

Table 6.3. Built-in functions of FORTRAN IV involving complex numbers.
  The functions AIMAG, CABS, and REAL are real functions of a complex
  argument. CMPLX is a complex function of two real arguments. The
       remainder are complex functions of a complex argument.

PROBLEM 6.4:   The discrete Fourier transform of a series of N real numbers X_0, X_1,...,X_{N-1} is given by

$$Y_n = \frac{1}{N} \sum_{k=0}^{N-1} X_k \, e^{-\frac{j2\pi kn}{N}} \qquad \text{for } n = 0,1,\ldots,N-1$$

where Y_n is complex. Write a complex function subprogram to provide Y_n for a given real array X of length N and a particular n.

The inverse transform

$$X_k = \sum_{n=0}^{N-1} Y_n \, e^{\frac{j2\pi kn}{N}} \qquad \text{for } k = 0,1,\ldots,N-1$$

should convert the complex array Y of length N containing all the results Y_0, Y_1,...,Y_{N-1} back into the real number X_k. Write a real function subprogram to do this given the complex array Y, length N, and a particular k.

5 Rules Governing Combination of Variable Types

The main types of FORTRAN variable have now been covered and it is the purpose of this section to summarize in tabular form the rules governing their combination.

(i)   Logical expressions can consist of combinations of logical variables, logical operators, and relational expressions. The rules for forming these and the hierarchy of operations were described in Chapter 6, Section 1.

(ii)   Arithmetic expressions involving addition, subtraction, multiplication, and division allow the combinations of variable type shown in Fig. 6.10.

(iii)   Exponentiation in arithmetic expressions can only be done with the combinations of variable type shown in Fig. 6.11.

(iv)   Assignment of values to variables in arithmetic statements can only be done for the types of conversion shown in Fig. 6.12.

Addition, Subtraction, Multiplication, Division

	Real	Integer	Double precision	Complex	Logical
Real	YES	▨	YES	YES	▨
Integer	▨	YES	▨	▨	▨
Double precision	YES	▨	YES	▨	▨
Complex	YES	▨	▨	YES	▨
Logical	▨	▨	▨	▨	▨

Fig. 6.10. Allowed combinations of variable type for the arithmetic operations of addition, subtraction, multiplication, and division. Note that integers may only be combined with integers, and both complex and double precision can be combined with themselves or with reals, but not with each other. Logical variables cannot be used for arithmetic at all.

Exponentiation : base $**$ exponent

Exponent

Base		Real	Integer	Double precision	Complex	Logical
	Real	YES	YES	YES	▨	▨
	Integer	▨	YES	▨	▨	▨
	Double precision	YES	YES	YES	▨	▨
	Complex	▨	YES	▨	▨	▨
	Logical	▨	▨	▨	▨	▨

Fig. 6.11. Allowed combinations of variable type for the exponentiation operation. Note that integers or complex may only be raised to integer powers. Real and double precision may be raised to real, integer, or double precision power. Logical variables cannot be used for arithmetic at all.

Variable = expression

expression type

	Real	Integer	Double precision	Complex	Logical
Real	YES	YES	YES		
Integer	YES	YES	YES		
Double precision	YES	YES	YES		
Complex	YES			YES	
Logical					YES

variable type

Fig. 6.12. Allowed conversions in arithmetic assignment statements. If the expression contains any complex variables or constants then it is of type complex. If it contains any double precision variables or constants then it is of type double precision. Real, integer, or double precision results can be converted to each other in any combination. Complex variables can be assigned only real or complex results; note that a real variable cannot be assigned a complex result. Logical types may not be converted.

The type statements of FORTRAN are among those included in the recommended order of statements at the beginning of programs. Refer to Chapter 5, Section 9 for the recommended arrangement.

6 The Use of EXTERNAL Variables

The final type of special variable in FORTRAN is the external variable, and it represents a somewhat different concept from all the other variable types. All other types of variable are used in situations where their names stand for numerical (or logical) values stored in the computer memory, and the names given to variables in a program or subprogram are known only locally in that particular program module. When variables are shared, it is done either through dummy arguments or the use of common, and it is the values taken by the variables which matter. Even with common, where space is shared between modules, the actual names used are not important - the values are identified by their position in common storage and different names can be used to refer to the same value.

External variables are used (not very often) in the one situation where the actual name of a variable is the message. This is where the name of a function or subroutine is to be communicated to a subprogram as an argument.

A name can be made known outside the local program by the EXTERNAL statement:

EXTERNAL *names*

This statement signifies that the names do not stand for values, but are instead the actual names of functions or subroutines, and that these *names* may be passed as arguments of a subprogram. The EXTERNAL statement is order-dependent like any other type statement. A name which appears in an EXTERNAL statement can only be the name of a subprogram and so it cannot be dimensioned by the EXTERNAL statement itself, and it cannot appear in COMMON, DIMENSION, or EQUIVALENCE statements. However it can appear in another type statement which defines the type of the function subprogram names. If, for example, SHAPE were an external variable which was the name of an integer function, then it should appear in both EXTERNAL and INTEGER statements:

        INTEGER SHAPE
        EXTERNAL SHAPE

EXAMPLE: A programmer decides to write a real function TRIG to evaluate trigonometric functions of any angle given in degrees. It is used by giving the desired function name and the angle as arguments of TRIG.

The subprogram TRIG is then:

```
FUNCTION TRIG(FUNC,ANGL)
EXTERNAL FUNC
XANGL=ANGL*ATAN(1.∅)/(45.∅)
TRIG=FUNC(ANGL)
RETURN
END
```

In a main program containing the statements:

```
EXTERNAL SIN
    .
    .
    .
X=TRIG(SIN,3∅.∅)
    .
    .
    .
```

the value of the sine of 30° would be found using TRIG. The external variable FUNC in the subroutine acts as a dummy argument in the usual way, except that it is a subprogram name which is passed, in this case SIN.

PROBLEM 6.5: Write a subroutine for numerical quadrature by Simpson's rule (Problem 4.8) of a function which is named as a dummy argument in the subroutine call:

$$\text{CALL SIMP(X0,X1,NSTEP,FUNC,ANS)}$$

where   X0 = lower limit of integration
        X1 = upper limit of integration
     NSTEP = number of strips into which to divide the interval
             (X0,X1). NSTEP should be even
      FUNC = the name of the function to be evaluated
       ANS = the result of the integration

Using function subprograms to evaluate the functions, find to an accuracy of 0.1%

(i) $0.5 + \dfrac{1}{2\pi}\displaystyle\int_0^1 e^{-x^2/2}\,dx$ (Answer 0.8413)

(ii) $\displaystyle\int_0^{\pi/2} \dfrac{dx}{\sqrt{1 - \dfrac{\sin^2 x}{4}}}$ (Answer 1.686)

7 Input and Output

1 Introduction

A certain amount of basic information about input and output under control of the FORMAT statement was introduced gradually as it became necessary in using FORTRAN and in solving problems. The purpose of this chapter is to summarize the techniques already mentioned and to introduce the remaining facilities.

The reader will be familiar by now with the meaning of the terms input and output. When a computer program through a READ statement demands values of data, then to satisfy this demand input is given to the computer on cards, teletype, magnetic tape, or other medium. When the program undertakes through a WRITE, PRINT, or PUNCH statement to provide values to the outside world, then the action is called output.

Another item of terminology will be useful here, called a record. A record is the basic unit of input or output. A printed line of output is a record; so too is a single card of input. However records need not be fixed in length. Whenever a READ or WRITE statement occurs, a new record of input or output begins. Within a formatted read or write statement new lines of information occasionally begin as described earlier by the nature of the FORMAT specification. Each new line is also a new record. As will be seen this term becomes particularly useful when dealing with unformatted information in which case the words line or card would not apply.

2 Formatted READ and WRITE statements

The fundamental input and output statements of FORTRAN are the READ and WRITE statements although for the purposes of output PUNCH and PRINT are equivalent to WRITE. The statements are

        READ(n,m) $list$
        WRITE(n,m) $list$
        PUNCHm, $list$
        PRINTm, $list$

where *n* can be a variable or constant, and *m* is a statement number.
All begin a formatted input or output operation in which the FORTRAN
variables named in the *list* are transferred from or to unit *n**
according to the FORMAT statement *m* which must be present in the
program. This protocol should be familiar enough at this stage to
make a detailed explanation unnecessary. Although the PUNCH and
PRINT statements are new, their functions are readily seen to be
punching cards or printing on paper. It is obvious therefore that
their unit number *n* is not required.

A variation of these statements is described in Section 8 of this
chapter, the NAMELIST statement which can be used in place of FORMAT.
With NAMELIST as an exception, the *list* given by the input/output
statements is a list of variable names separated by commas. In the
formatted case it is important to be sure exactly how many data
values are implied by the *list* because these must be matched exactly
by the FORMAT specification *m*. If the *list* consists of ordinary
scalar variables of type real, integer, logical, or double precision
there is no problem, the number of data values transmitted is just
the number of items in the *list*.

EXAMPLE:

        READ(5,21)X,Y,I,J

As long as the variables X, Y, I, J are each either real, integer,
logical, or double precision the input request is for four values
which are to be provided on unit 5 according to the FORMAT statement numbered 21.

If complex numbers are involved, then care has to be taken to
provide two values for each complex pair. Remember that both numbers
in the pair are themselves real; there is no such thing as a complex
integer.

EXAMPLE:

        REAL P,Q,R
        LOGICAL Y
        COMPLEX C,S
             :
             :
        PRINT 25,P,C,Q,Y,R,S

Eight values are printed according to the FORMAT numbered 25.

---

* Tradition has ordained tape 5 as the usual unit of input from cards and
  tape 6 as output to a printer. Naturally there are local variations.

With arrays the *list* can either give a subscript in which case it
is clear that a single value is intended, or it can name the array
causing all of it to be transmitted.

EXAMPLE:

```
INTEGER MOM,DAD
COMPLEX KIDS
DIMENSION KIDS(3),XRAY(3,2)
PUNCH 21, MOM,DAD,KIDS,XRAY(1,1)
```

Here nine values are punched on cards - the integer values MOM and
DAD, six real values representing the complex array KIDS, and the
real value XRAY(1,1).

With multidimensional arrays it is important to know in what order
the information is transmitted. Unfortunately it is not in the most
obvious or convenient order. Perhaps the inventors of FORTRAN were
mathematically illiterate, because arrays are transmitted with the
first subscript varying most rapidly. For two dimensional arrays
this means to a mathematician that the order of transmission is by
columns meaning the transpose of what might be expected. The usual
notation for an array of dimensions mxn is

$$
\begin{matrix}
a_{11} & a_{12} & a_{13} & \cdots & a_{1n} \\
a_{21} & a_{22} & a_{23} & \cdots & a_{2n} \\
\vdots & & & & \\
a_{m1} & a_{m2} & a_{m3} & \cdots & a_{mn}
\end{matrix}
$$

The FORTRAN statements

```
DIMENSION A(5,4)
READ (5,21) A
```

cause the 25 items of real data to be read down the columns:

$$a_{11}, a_{21}, a_{31}, a_{41}, a_{51}, a_{12}, \cdots \text{ etc}$$

This in itself is not so bad, but consider the statement

```
   PRINT(27) A
27 FORMAT(1X,5F10.5)
```

which will produce the highly confusing paper result:

$$a_{11} \quad a_{21} \quad a_{31} \quad a_{41} \quad a_{51}$$

$$a_{12} \quad a_{22} \quad a_{32} \quad a_{42} \quad a_{52}$$

$$a_{13} \quad a_{23} \quad a_{33} \quad a_{43} \quad a_{53}$$

$$a_{14} \quad a_{24} \quad a_{34} \quad a_{44} \quad a_{54}$$

Remember carefully that FORTRAN reads array variables with the first subscript varying most rapidly;   that is to say in column order.

Finally, the effects of the above can be mitigated by use of the implied DO-loop facility which allows blocks from arrays to be selected.   The syntax must be exact as chosen complete with apparently redundant brackets from the following example:

```
DIMENSION P(1Ø),Q(1Ø 1Ø),R(1Ø,1Ø,1Ø)
     :
     :

PRINT 25,(P(I),I=1,5),((Q(I,J),J=1,5),I=1,5)
PRINT 25,(((R(I,J,K),K=1,5),J=1,5),I=1,5)
```

Of course the choice of variables and limits and their order is optional;   it is the punctuation that is rigid.   To return to the earlier example, the following is the sensible way of keeping a matrix straight and is the usual practice:

```
DIMENSION A(5,5)
     :
     :

   WRITE(6,51) ((A(I,J),J=1,3),I=1,3)
51 FORMAT(1X,3F1Ø.5)
```

This prints the desired submatrix in the order

$$a_{11} \quad a_{12} \quad a_{13}$$

$$a_{21} \quad a_{22} \quad a_{23}$$

$$a_{31} \quad a_{32} \quad a_{33}$$

For, comparison, the statement

```
   PRINT 25,A
25 FORMAT(1X,5F1Ø.5)
```

is the equivalent of

        PRINT 25((A(I,J),I=1,5),J=1,5)

An implied DO-loop can contain several variables, and they need not all be subscripted. The statement

        WRITE(6,9Ø)(X,A(I), (B(I,J),J=1,3),I=1,4)
     9Ø FORMAT(1X,5F1Ø.5)

is valid and the arrangement of the output is:

$$x \quad a_1 \quad b_{11} \quad b_{12} \quad b_{13}$$

$$x \quad a_2 \quad b_{21} \quad b_{22} \quad b_{23}$$

$$x \quad a_3 \quad b_{31} \quad b_{32} \quad b_{33}$$

$$x \quad a_4 \quad b_{41} \quad b_{42} \quad b_{43}$$

This assumes that X is a scalar, A is an array of one dimension whose length is at least 4, and B is in two dimensions of at least 4 x 3. It is even possible to have

        WRITE(6,11ØØ)(I,A(I),I=1,3)

but watch out for

        READ(5,22)(K,B(K),I=1,12)
or
        READ(5,22)(K,B(I),I=1,K)

which are legal but tricky, particularly the second.

3 FORMAT Specifications

   The input and output statements described in the previous section refer to FORMAT statements for information about how the values are to be presented. As has been described earlier, a FORMAT statement consists of field descriptions of the data that is expected and of other punctuation which can be commas to separate fields, parentheses (brackets) to divide up the specification, and slashes to indicate new lines or records. FORMAT statements are not executed by the program in the same way as, for example, is a WRITE statement. They may therefore be placed virtually anywhere in the program after the order dependent set and before END. Any number of different READ and WRITE statements may refer to the same FORMAT. A FORMAT statement will always have a statement number and takes the form:

statement number FORMAT (*specification*)

and the *specification* breaks down into

field punctuation field punctuation ...

The field types must exist in one-to-one correspondence with the variables called for by the *list* given by the input/output statements. First the available field types are described here.

(a) Integer

A field of the form

$$n I m$$

calls for n consecutive integers each occupying m spaces and each right justified in the m spaces. Sufficient space must be given for the values expected and if the number is negative its sign counts as a space. The treatment of the I specification is identical for input and output.

EXAMPLE: The statements

```
      DATA I,J,K,L/-99,Ø,75,1Ø23/
      WRITE(6,2Ø)L,K,J,I
   2Ø FORMAT(2I5,I2,I4)
```

will produce the printed line

```
 1Ø23    75 Ø -99
```

(b) Real without exponent—F

The field

$$k F \ell . j$$

specifies k real numbers in ℓ spaces each with j decimal places. ℓ must of course be greater than j to allow room for the decimal point and possibly for a negative sign as well. For output using WRITE, PRINT or PUNCH statements the number is transmitted in exactly the stated specification. For input using READ the field width ℓ is obeyed exactly but if a decimal point is given the data can be moved about within the field. If the input data does not contain a decimal point, one is provided for it before the last *j* digits.

EXAMPLE: The real value 3.14 is to be read as follows:

        READ(5,15)X
    15 FORMAT(F5.2)

The information could be provided on unit 5 with the decimal point implied as

  . 314
  · · · · ·

or with it given explicitly as either

  3.14
  · · · · ·

or

3.14
· · · · ·

Were it written out again by

WRITE(6,15)X

it would invariably appear as

  3.14
  · · · · ·

As a bonus, it is usually possible to give an E-formatted data value in response to a READ inside the field where an F is called for. Or vice versa.

(c) Real with exponent—E

The specification

$$kEm.n$$

calls for *k* repetitions of a field *m* digits wide with *n* decimal places and an exponent. A number represented in this way contains many symbols in addition to the digits themselves. *m* must therefore be greater than *n* by at least 7. The printed E field comes out as

$$s\emptyset.\underbrace{ddd...dd}_{} \; \underbrace{Esdd}_{}$$

             n digits   exponent
             mantissa

where *s* is a sign and *d* are digits.

EXAMPLES: Using a field E15.5 the following numbers would be printed as shown.

number	printed output
3×10^{10}	$0.30000E\ 11$
16.35×10^{-4}	$0.16350E-02$
-7.32×10^{24}	$-0.73200E\ 25$
-4.28×10^{-15}	$-0.42800E-14$

As with F fields, FORTRAN allows some slight variations on the exact alignment of input data.   First of all the information which is to be read in E form can be moved about within the field of m spaces, and as long as the decimal point and exponent are given no trouble will be encountered.   Therefore the number 3×10^{10} could be read in by the statements:

       READ(5,21)X
    21 FORMAT(E15.5)

in several ways including:

     0.30000E 11
       3.0E10
           3.E10

The letter E can be left out as long as the sign of the exponent (+ or -) is included:

     3.0+10
         3.+10

The decimal point can also be left out, but then it is assumed to precede *n* digits of the mantissa:

         30000E 11
    300000+10

Again it is often legal to substitute a value in F form in response to a READ statement which is expecting an E number in the particular field.

(d) Complex Numbers

   Since a complex number is a pair of real numbers, two real fields, or one real field repeated, are the correct FORMAT specification to correspond to a complex number in the *list*.

(e) Double Precision Numbers—D

A specification

$$kDm.n$$

is used for the input or output of k double precision numbers, which
is similar to the E format. m is the total field width and n the
number of digits printed after the decimal place. An exponent is
always printed, just as in an E field, and so m must be at least 7
greater than n. Real and double precision fields are not interchangeable. When a double precision number is printed the D specification is followed exactly. For input the same variations in the
layout of the data are permitted as for E conversion except that the
letter D is used. Often the exponent can be omitted so that the
input resembles a real number with a decimal point given.

(f) Logical Values—L

In a FORMAT statement logical values are indicated by

$$kLn$$

where there are k logical variables to be transmitted, each occupying
a field of n spaces. For output the letter T for .TRUE. and F for
.FALSE. appears right justified in the field. On input the first
nonblank character in the field is expected to be either T or F and
the remainder of the field is ignored.

(g) Octal Fields—O

All the numbers considered before have been decimal, but computers
actually work in the binary system. Frequently a programmer may
wish to see the binary equivalent of his data, but a binary number
of even modest size is very long. The octal number system is a very
convenient one for transmitting binary information because the mental
conversion into binary is very simple.

EXAMPLE: The number 37 in decimal is 100101 in binary and 45 in
octal. The octal version simply represents groups of three binary
digits as one octal digit, i.e.

100101
4   5

The complete octal to binary table is

Octal	Binary
0	000
1	001
2	010
3	011
4	100
5	101
6	110
7	111

and the next octal number is 10, corresponding to 8 in decimal notation or 1000 in binary.

The FORMAT specification (if allowed)

$$k0n$$

allows k numbers to be printed in the octal system with a field width of n octal digits. The input/output *list* could specify either real or integer variables, and any other type could be accessed by means of the EQUIVALENCE facility. It will be found that integer values will translate directly into their octal equivalent, but surprises are in store with all other types.

(h) Hexadecimal fields—Z

On some computers the organization of the machine is based on 8-bit segments called "bytes". In such a system the binary equivalent in octal does not fit an eight bit segment because each octal digit represents three binary bits; eight is not a multiple of three. Hexadecimal (base 16) notation is used to fit an 8-bit byte but in order to count to 15 using single digits our number system is extended using letters. Hexadecimal to binary conversion operates as:

Hexadecimal	Binary
0	0000
1	0001
2	0010
3	0011
4	0100
5	0101
6	0110
7	0111
8	1000
9	1001
A	1010
B	1011
C	1100
D	1101
E	1110
F	1111

and the next hexadecimal number is 10, corresponding to 16 in decimal or 10000 in binary. Two hexadecimal digits make up one 8-bit byte.

The FORMAT specification (if allowed)

$$kZn$$

calls for k numbers to be printed in thin hexadecimal form as n hexadecimal digits; this can be done for either real or integer variables and extended to all types using EQUIVALENCE.

(i) Alphanumeric fields and data—A or H

A-fields are used to read or write alphanumeric variables, and an H-field is an alphanumeric constant. H-conversion will already be familiar from earlier sections. The field

$$nHmessage$$

in a FORMAT introduces alphanumeric information (meaning letters and numbers) which can be printed (or read in which case a new message is required to replace the one given). The *message* must follow the letter H and contained in exactly n spaces following it which are reserved for the message. The example was

```
    WRITE(6,66)
  6 FORMAT(13H HELLO SAILOR)
```

Some computers allow an H-conversion to be used elsewhere in a program just as if it were an alphanumeric constant.

The A-conversion feature is one which allows alphanumeric data to be written or read using variable names. Corresponding to either a real or integer variable, the FORMAT statement can contain

$$kAn$$

which specifies that k sets of alphanumeric fields are required, each of n characters. For input any alphanumeric message can be read and it can be written out again. Indeed much more can be done, as follows.

First of all either integer or real variables can be used to store alphanumeric data. Therefore the following programs are valid, which read in a four letter word and print it out again. Note that both use the same FORMAT.

```
      READ(5,31)WORD
      WRITE(6,31)WORD
   31 FORMAT(1X,A4)
```

or

```
      READ(5,31)MESS
      WRITE(6,31)MESS
   31 FORMAT(1X,A4)
```

It is possible to use variables which have alphanumeric information assigned to them in any statement of FORTRAN, with care. They make very little sense in alphanumeric expressions, but it can be useful to use them in arithmetic statements as long as the type is not changed. For example, the following will transfer its message from a variable X to a variable Y assuming both are real.

```
      READ(5,31)X
      Y=X
      WRITE(6,31)Y
   31 FORMAT(1X,A4)
```

This is exactly the same as the previous two examples because X and Y are the same type and so the data in X is transferred directly into Y with no conversion. If however one tried:

```
      READ(5,31)X
      I=X
      WRITE(6,31)I
   31 FORMAT(1X,A4)
```

the attempted conversion from real to integer ruins the data. Therefore alphanumeric information can be used in either real or integer
expressions so long as the program does not at any time attempt a
conversion. Any attempt to manipulate alphanumeric data by an
arithmetic calculation also affects the message although in a few
far-fetched situations a programmer might accomplish shifting and OR-
ing by arithmetic means.

   If two messages are compared by an IF statement, then the computer
compares the bit patterns of the messages and this could be useful,
although it requires some care. First of all in this case the
variables ought to be integers so the system cannot try to be clever
about decimal points and exponents in the comparison. Secondly the
message ought not to involve the sign bit of the data word and so
this is clearly a job for an expert. Within these constraints, it
is possible to sort words into alphabetical order. Here is a simple
program to do this which assumes at least *four* letters fit into a
data location and sorts an array of *three* letter words into alphabetic order.

```
      DIMENSION IWD(1Ø)
C     READ IN THE WORDS
      WRITE(6,2Ø)
   2Ø FORMAT(36H PROVIDE 1Ø THREE LETTER WORDS, 1ØA4)
      READ(5,21)IWD
   21 FORMAT(1ØA4)
C     SORT INTO ALPHABETIC ORDER
      DO 3Ø K=1,9
      LMIN=K+1
      DO 3Ø L=LMIN,1Ø
C     COMPARE TWO WORDS
      IF(IWD(K).LT.IWD(L))GO TO 3Ø
C     INTERCHANGE THE TWO
      JWD=IWD(K)
      IWD(K)=IWD(L)
      IWD(L)=JWD
   3Ø CONTINUE
```

This program clearly has wider applications and uses a method known
as bubble sorting. After the first pass, with K=1, the smallest
value is certain to be in IWD(1), after the second pass the second

smallest will be in IWD(2) and so on. Note how the interchange uses
the variable JWD to save IWD(K) temporarily. The method relies on
the letters of the alphabet having a "code" which is in ascending
order. This is usually the case but depends on the computer system.

It is possible to assign an alphanumeric message to a variable in
a DATA statement. Simply put the message as an H specification in
the DATA statement.

EXAMPLE:

        DATA DOT,STAR/1H.,1H*/

This will be very useful in graph plotting as will be seen. This
is the only way of doing this in a DATA statement. The nonstandard
FORMAT feature described below in (j) cannot be used.

Finally there is the question of how many letters of a message can
be put into one data word*. The answer depends on the computer
system, its word length, and the type of character used. Suppose the
number is 4. Then a message longer than 4 characters will occupy
more than one data value and so an array may be necessary.

EXAMPLE: Assuming 4 letters per computer location, the message in
    the following program requires an array of four words

```
        DIMENSION CHEEKY(4)
        DATA CHEEKY/13H HELLO SAILOR/
        WRITE(6,21)CHEEKY
     21 FORMAT(4A4)
```

The message does not completely fill the fourth location, so the
computer fills the message out with trailing blanks. Incomplete
locations are always filled out with additional trailing blanks
when reading or defining alphanumeric data.

Note carefully that the integer value 123 is not the same as the
message "123", i.e. in the following data statement I and J are
nothing like one another:

        DATA I,J/123,3H123/

---

* Generally 16 or 32 bit computers use 2 and 4 respectively, ie one character
  for each 8 bits. Sometimes there is one letter for each 6 bits as on 60
  bit machines which hold 10 characters per word.

(j) Literal Messages

Some computer systems allow a message to be defined in a FORMAT statement without the need to count the letters in the message as in the H specification. This feature is not part of standard FORTRAN but is widespread enough in use to be well worth knowing. Simply enclose the message in single quotation marks:

```
      WRITE(6,39)
   39 FORMAT(' THIS IS A LITERAL MESSAGE')
```

The literal message cannot itself contain a quotation mark; the only way to include one in to use the normal H-field. This type of message can be used in FORMAT statements. A few compilers used to allow an asterisk (*) instead of a quotation mark (') but this practice is dying out.

(k) Blank fields—X

The specification

$$nX$$

introduces n spaces into a line of input or output. On input n characters are ignored and on output n blanks are produced. It was emphasised earlier, and will be again, that it is essential to begin each line on a line-printer with a blank, usually as 1X.

(l) Punctuation by commas

When a FORMAT contains a number of fields, these are usually separated by commas in the absence of other punctuation; it is safest to do this always.

EXAMPLE:

```
   66 FORMAT(1X,7HMESSAGE,3I5,2F6.0)
```

Sometimes the commas are not necessary. In the above example two could be omitted because there would be no ambiguity as a result:

```
   66 FORMAT(1X7MESSAGE3I5,2F6.0)
```

Clearly the readability is affected. The remaining comma is necessary to separate 5 from the 2.

(m) Punctuation by brackets—repetitions

To facilitate repetitions of FORMAT groups, FORTRAN allows a limited
depth of paired brackets which may be provided by an integer repetition
constant.

EXAMPLE:

    127 FORMAT(1X,5(F1∅.5,I3))

takes care of 5 pairs of real and integer variables in a line of
66 spaces.

The maximum depth allowed is

    91 FORMAT((( )))

If the *list* of an input/output statement is not finished when the end
of a FORMAT statement is encountered, then the specification is
repeated *on a new line* from the first embedded bracket using its
repetition factor. The statements

        DIMENSION UNIT(3,3)
        DATA UNIT/1.,3*∅.,1.,3*∅,1./
        WRITE(6,975)((UNIT(I,J),J=I,3),I=1,3)
    975 FORMAT(3(1X,3F5.2))

write the matrix on three lines in row order (although this is one
of the few cases where the order does not matter since the array is
symmetric). If there are no embedded brackets it repeats from the
beginning.

(n) Punctuation by slashes—new lines

A FORMAT can call for a new line to begin by using a slash (/).
Every READ, WRITE, PUNCH, or PRINT statement starts with a new line,
and due to the nature of the FORMAT other new lines may occur if the
whole FORMAT is repeated.

EXAMPLE: In the previous example a message could be written before
the matrix and could be spaced out by additional blank lines:

    975 FORMAT(1X,13HA UNIT MATRIX//3(1X,3F5.2/))

which will generate:

A UNIT MATRIX

1.ØØ Ø.ØØ Ø.ØØ
Ø.ØØ 1.ØØ Ø.ØØ
Ø.ØØ Ø.ØØ 1.ØØ

(o) Scale factors—P

Data to be printed or read can be scaled by a power of 10 make its range more convenient. For input it is restricted to use with F format, and the real data can be multiplied by 10^{-n} where n is the scale constant. It is written as a field

$$nP$$

and once established affects all F fields which occur later in the same FORMAT, even if the FORMAT is repeated.

EXAMPLE: Suppose real data is in a field

ddd.ddd

but for some reason the programmer wishes to move the decimal point two places left, i.e. to interpret the numbers as d.ddddd. The format

11 FORMAT(2PF7.3)

will do this.

For output, P-scaling affects all following F, E, or D fields. It should be noted therefore that a FORMAT with P in it is treated differently for input and output. On output the scaling is the opposite, i.e. the printed data is first multiplied by 10^n. Thus the statements

READ(5,11)X

and then

WRITE(6,11)X

using the earlier FORMAT (2PF7.3) would read 123.456 as 1.23456 and later print it as 123.456 again (assuming X had not been modified by the program).

(p) Records and unit numbers

In the introduction to this chapter an attempt was made to explain the notion of records. Now it is possible to be more explicit for formatted data. Effectively a record is a line. Thus each new READ, WRITE, PRINT, or PUNCH statement begins a new record, but more than one record could be produced if the FORMAT is repeated or if slashes are encountered. The total number of records is the total number of lines. The allowed length of a record will depend on the physical device involved. A card reader can only provide 80 columns and similarly a card punch can only punch the first 80 characters of the record. Since in either case a new card is only begun when a new record is called for, it is up to the programmer to organize his "card images" correctly.

Lineprinters are often wider - 130 columns is a standard width. And other devices can be used, which is why the input/output statements have unit numbers to refer to. Unit 5 is often a card reader and unit 6 a printer. But units 1-4, and 7 onwards could well exist as tape drives, disks, or other useful devices. The general ideas of units and records apply to all devices. Therefore programs can read and write using a variety of types of equipment.

(q) Carriage Control

As has been mentioned, the first column of output has special meaning if the output device is a lineprinter. Up to now it has been suggested that the first column should be left blank because the printer then advances one line before printing. Other options are:

First Character	Meaning
blank	print on the next line
0	double space (next line but one)
1	new page
+	print on the same line

If the number 1 sneaks into the first column of output by mistake, a lot of paper can be wasted. The + feature can be useful for graph plotting as will be seen.

(r) Object time FORMAT

This rather mysterious title refers to the ability to actually read in the FORMAT when a program is running rather than defining it in the program. It is possible for two reasons; first of all FORTRAN allows a variable to be used as the FORMAT address and secondly FORMAT specifications are stored in the computer in symbolic form (i.e. just like the message) and are decoded as the program runs*.

To use it, it is necessary to DIMENSION an array which will hold the FORMAT as an alphanumeric message and is long enough to do so. Even if only one location is required a DIMENSION (of 1) must be given. The desired FORMAT can then be read in and should be just like a FORMAT statement without the word FORMAT - it should begin and end with the outer parentheses (brackets). It can then be used as a FORMAT. The following example assumes 4 characters per computer word.

EXAMPLE:

```
      DIMENSION IFORM(2∅)
      READ(5,1)IFORM
    1 FORMAT(2∅A4)
```

This reads into the array IFORM a FORMAT specification which could later be used as a FORMAT:

```
      READ(5,IFORM)X,Y,Z
```

The given FORMAT on unit 5 could be

```
 (3F1∅.5)
```

4 FORMAT Free Input and Output

Standard FORTRAN IV does not support this facility, but something similar has been included in many timesharing systems. The terms "FORMAT Free" or "Free FORMAT" do not mean the same as "Unformatted" which is standard feature described in a later section.

---

* Some programming languages operate this way: the program is stored in essentially its original form and is *interpreted* by an *interpreter* program from the original as it is executed, rather than being *compiled* into machine language before execution as FORTRAN is. Interpretive languages usually execute slowly.

The statements

> READ,*list*

or

> READ*,*list*

ask for a number of variables to be provided from the standard input device, either a card reader or in a timesharing system a teletype. The data can be provided free of FORMAT constraints, as a series of numbers with commas between but still carefully in one-to-one correspondence by type; reals must have their decimal points and integers must not.

Similarly the statements

> PRINT, *list*

or

> PRINT*, *list*

will produce printed results but the programmer has no control over their spacing. Messages in H-fields can be included in *list*.

5 Graph Plotting

Some of the facilities of input and output in FORTRAN can be combined to plot graphs in two ways, based on implied DO-loops in the first case and on alphanumeric arrays in the second. One line-printers (but not teletypes) the "no space" carriage control (+) can be used to overstrike. These facilities are best described by a series of examples.

EXAMPLE: This program plots a single graph of the function

$$f(x) = \frac{1}{\sqrt{2\pi}} e^{-x^2/2}$$

which is actually the probability density function of the standard normal distribution with zero mean and unit variance. The function is defined in an arithmetic statement function and the blank and asterisk used to plot the graph are established in a DATA statement. The implied DO-loop in the WRITE statement controls the number of blanks printed and so the position of the asterisk. The

FORMAT specification 70A1 means that one space is allocated to each variable printed.

```
        DATA IPLUS,IBLANK,ISTAR/1H+,1H ,1H*/
        GAUSS(X)=EXP(-X*X/2.Ø)
C       PLOT THE Y-AXIS
        WRITE(6,2Ø)(IPLUS,K=1,45)
   2Ø   FORMAT(1X,7ØA1)
        C=1.Ø/SQRT(8.Ø*ATAN(1.Ø))
        DO 5Ø L=1,2Ø
C CALCULATE AND PLOT THE FUNCTION VALUES
        IPLACE=GAUSS(FLOAT(L)/1Ø.Ø)*4Ø.Ø-Ø.5
        WRITE(6,2Ø)IPLUS,(IBLANK,K=1,IPLACE),ISTAR
   5Ø   CONTINUE
        STOP
        END
```

The output from this program is shown in Fig. 7.1.

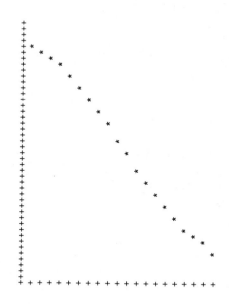

Fig.7.1. Printed output from a graph plotting program.

EXAMPLE: Using much the same approach, a histogram can be prepared.
A function RANF(0.) gives random numbers whose expected distribution is rectangular, i.e. uniform between 0.0 and 1.0. Fig. 7.2
is the probability density function. In reality the subroutine
should not give an exactly flat histogram for a finite number of
tries - if it did it would be very suspicious because it is supposed
to be random. Suppose IHIST is the array in which the histogram
is arranged before plotting. The number of trials is variable as
is the number of bins up to a maximum of 1000.

```
      DIMENSION IHIST(1001)
      DATA ISTAR/1H*/
C DEFINE THE PARAMETERS
      WRITE(6,10)
   10 FORMAT(35H PROVIDE THE NO. OF BINS TO USE, I4)
      READ(5,20)N
   20 FORMAT(I4)
      WRITE(6,30)
   30 FORMAT(36H PROVIDE THE NO. OF TRIALS TO DO, I4)
      READ(5,20)M
C WORK OUT SCALING BASED ON EXPECTED NO. PER BIN
      S=40./(FLOAT(M)/FLOAT(N))
C INITIALIZE THE HISTOGRAM
      DO 40 K=1,N
   40 IHIST(K)=0
C OBTAIN M RANDOM NUMBERS AND FORM HISTOGRAM
      DO 60 K=1,M
C SCALE FROM 1 TO N
      L=IFIX(RANF(0.)*FLOAT(N)+1.)
C INCREMENT HISTOGRAM BIN
      IHIST(L)=IHIST(L)+1
   60 CONTINUE
C NOW PRINT THE HISTOGRAM
      DO 80 K=1,N
      ICOL=FLOAT(IHIST(K))*S
      WRITE(6,70)(ISTAR,L=1,ICOL)
   70 FORMAT(1X,70A1)
   80 CONTINUE
      STOP
      END
```

A typical output from this program is shown in Fig. 7.3.

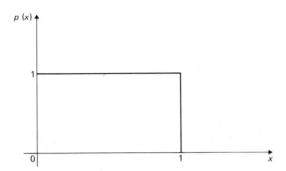

Fig.7.2. Probability density function for a rectangular distribution.

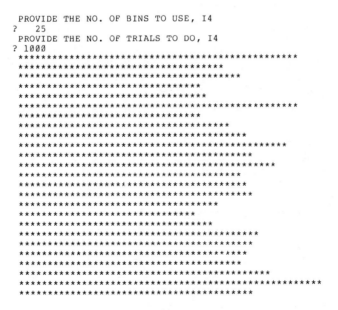

Fig.7.3. Printed histogram of 1000 numbers from a rectangular distribution.

EXAMPLE: A graph which has several symbols per line can be done in the same way very easily on a lineprinter using the overprint carriage control. Here is a program which prints a cycle of sin(x) and cos(x) together.

```
          DATA IBL,IS,IC,II/1H ,1HS,1HC,1HI/
          CON=8.0*ATAN(1.0)
          DO 60 K=1,25
          X=FLOAT(K-1)*CON/24.0
    C CALCULATE AND PRINT THE SINE
          IPLACE=26.5+25.0*SIN(X)
          WRITE(6,10)(IBL,L=1,IPLACE),IS
       10 FORMAT(1X,80A1)
    C CALCULATE AND PRINT THE COSINE ON SAME LINE
          IPLACE=26.5+25.0*COS(X)
          WRITE(6,20)(IBL,L=1,IPLACE),IC
          WRITE(6,20)(IBL,L=1,25),II
       20 FORMAT(1H+,80A1)
       60 CONTINUE
          STOP
          END
```

The graph is shown in Fig. 7.4.

EXAMPLE: It may not be possible to use the overprint carriage control; on a timesharing terminal it is certain not to be available. One could write a complicated program which sorted out in which order the printing must be done with many special cases. Alternatively an array can be used to construct the line before it is printed, and this would be the usual method. Here is the same example done this way:

```
          DIMENSION ILINE(70)
          DATA IBL,IS,IC,II/1H ,1HS,1HC,1HI/
          CON=8.0*ATAN(1.0)
       10 FORMAT(1X,70A1)
          DO 60 K=1,25
          X = FLOAT(K-1)*CON/24.0
    C CLEAR THE LINE
          DO 20 L=1,70
       20 ILINE(L)=IBL
    C CALCULATE PRINT POSITION OF BOTH FUNCTIONS
          IPLS=26.5+25.0*SIN(X)
          IPLC=26.5+25.0*COS(X)
          ILINE(26)=II
          ILINE(IPLS)=IS
          ILINE(IPLC)=IC
          WRITE(6,10)ILINE
       60 CONTINUE
          STOP
          END
```

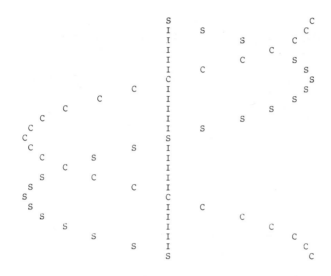

Fig.7.4. Printed graph using two symbols per line. There are two basic
methods for doing this.

PROBLEM 7.1: Write a subroutine to produce an isopotential diagram.
It accepts an array of two dimensions and produces a plot showing
the contours of equal values within the array as accurately as is
possible using printed lines, much like contour drawings on a
topographical map. Incorporate this subroutine into the solution
of Problem 5.11. Equal spacing of levels may not be the best
choice for displaying the results.

6 Manipulation of Input and Output Devices

The option of using a range of input/output devices is implicit in the READ and WRITE statements which provide for various unit numbers designated by the integer variable or constant *n*:

READ(*n,m*)*list*
WRITE(*n,m*)*list*

Clearly if these were the only operations available, their uses would be somewhat limited. However FORTRAN has three statements for device manipulation which are REWIND, BACKSPACE, and END FILE.

The most useful is the REWIND statement. At any time during processing a unit can be rewound either to start reading or writing again from the beginning. Unit *n* is rewound by the REWIND statement

REWIND *n*

where *n* is, as before, either an integer variable or constant:

REWIND 3

or

REWIND IUNIT

Neither the input file (usually unit 5) not the output file (usually unit 6) can be rewound, but a tape or disk file can be. When a unit is rewound to be rewritten, the new information destroys the old, and a word of caution is in order about tapes. A tape is a sequential access device, which is to say the computer starts from the beginning and writes consecutively before rewinding and reading or re-writing. But there is no guarantee on re-writing that the new information takes exactly the same physical space on the tape that the old information did *even if the FORMATs were identical*. This is because the physical characteristics of the device - its start and stop time and the actual density of information written on the tape will vary somewhat. So it is not safe to try to READ after WRITE without a REWIND. Put another way, if a unit is rewound and writing begins on it, it is best to consider *all* previous information to be lost.

EXAMPLE: Write, rewind, and re-read

```
      DO 31 K=1,1Ø
   31 WRITE(3,2Ø)K
   2Ø FORMAT(I1Ø)
      REWIND 3
      DO 32 K=1,1Ø
   32 READ(3,2Ø)K
```

EXAMPLE: Write, rewind, rewrite

```
   2Ø FORMAT(I1Ø)
      DO 31 K=1,1Ø
   31 WRITE(3,2Ø)K
      REWIND 3
      DO 32 K=1,2
   32 WRITE(3,2Ø)K
```

At this point it might be expected that a statement like

```
      READ(3,2Ø)I
```

would produce I=3. Well, it might but it is unsafe if unit 3 is a tape, as shown in Fig. 7.5. If unit 3 were a disk, then it could be done.

Once a unit has had information written on it and been rewound, the information can be reread but only by the exact equivalent READ and FORMAT statements to those used in writing it. Of course the variable names do not have to be the same, but the order of reading according to type and position must be exact because information can only be taken off in the order that it was put on. Furthermore, the organization into records must be compatible. Recall that every WRITE statement began a new record, and so does every READ statement. In the formatted case additional records are begun whenever the FORMAT is restarted or whenever a slash occurred.

EXAMPLE: Data is written according to

```
      DO 66 K=1,6
   66 WRITE(1,7Ø)I,J,X,Y
   7Ø FORMAT(2I1Ø,2F1Ø.5)
```

It can then only be recovered by compatible READ and FORMAT statements:

```
      REWIND 1
      DO 88 K=1,6
   88 READ(1,7Ø)L,M,W,Z
```

However because each READ statement begins a new record, partial records can be read:

```
      REWIND 1
      DO 91 K=1,6
   88 READ(1,95)L,M,W
   95 FORMAT(2I1Ø,F1Ø.5)
```

although the FORMAT statement 70 would have done just as well. The final real value in each record is passed over.

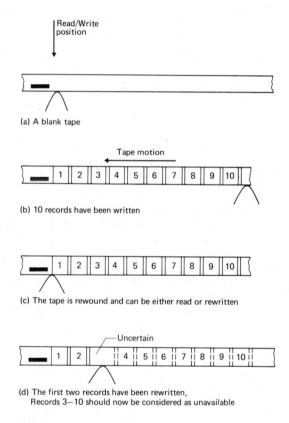

Fig.7.5. Manipulation of a tape using REWIND.

EXAMPLE: Data is written according to

        DIMENSION A(5,5)
             .
             .
             .
        WRITE(3,1∅)A
   1∅ FORMAT(25F5.∅)

and can be recovered by

        REWIND 3
        READ(3,1∅)A

EXAMPLE: Data is written by

        DIMENSION A(5,5)
             .
             .
             .
        WRITE(3,2∅)A
   2∅ FORMAT(5F5.∅)

and is contained in 5 records because of FORMAT repetition.   It
can then be reread by

        REWIND 3
        READ(3,2∅)A

or by

        REWIND 3
        DO 3∅ K=1,5
   3∅ READ(3,2∅)(A(L,K),L=1,5)

Note the order of subscripts.   The upper 3 x 3 part could be
accessed by

        REWIND 3
        DO 5∅ K=1,3
   5∅ READ(3,2∅)(A(L,K),L=1,3)

which is the only way to do this.   The last two elements of each
column are passed over because each time statement 50 is executed
a new record begins.

EXAMPLE: Data is written by

```
       WRITE(9,9Ø)X,Y,Z
    9Ø FORMAT(F1Ø.5,F5.2/F1Ø.5)
```

and is therefore in two records. It could be recovered by

```
       REWIND 9
       READ(9,9Ø)X,Y,Z
```

or by

```
       REWIND 9
       READ(9,91)X,Y
       READ(9,91)Z
    91 FORMAT(F1Ø.5,F5.2)
```

and finally X and Z alone could be obtained by

```
       REWIND 9
       READ(9,91)X
       READ(9,91)Z
```

The BACKSPACE *n* statement causes the unit to be stepped back *one record* on unit *n*. How far it steps back depends on the WRITE and FORMAT statements that produced it. It is possible to follow the sequence WRITE, BACKSPACE, READ but the next operation should not be READ on a tape for much the same reason as was described earlier. For a disk file this is not a problem. Be warned that computer manufacturers seem to have trouble in making this statement work correctly.

EXAMPLE: This is a permissible operation on tape or disk

```
       WRITE(9,9Ø)X,Y,Z
    9Ø FORMAT(F1Ø.5,F5.2/F1Ø.5)
       BACKSPACE 9
       READ(9,9Ø) P
```

what is read into P is the written value of Z. On a tape this cannot be followed by another READ.

The END FILE *n* statement causes a special mark to be written on the unit *n* signifying the end of a file of data. These special marks are sometimes used in data processing to separate groups of records of data. In FORTRAN it is not possible to read past an end-of-file mark under any circumstances. These marks are usually used in conjunction with special programs for skipping forward through data to a desired file. Since FORTRAN IV does not provide a way of doing this, these applications tend to be rather special.

7 Unformatted Input and Output

Another standard means of organising data on tape or disk files is by the use of unformatted input and output, which is not applicable to card readers, printers, or punches and should not be confused with the nonstandard Format-Free statements described earlier. Unformatted data is transferred in and out in a special code used by the computer system which is usually much more efficient in its use of tape or disk space and faster than formatted operations. It is simply arranged by using READ and WRITE statements without a FORMAT statement number:

        READ(n) *list*
        WRITE(n)*list*

These statements transfer the variables named in *list* to unit n in the unformatted form, sometimes called "binary records". With this kind of operation it is still true that each READ or WRITE statement begins a new record, but there is no way that extra new records can be started in the middle of *list*, so it is much easier to figure out the arrangement of records on a unit. It is still true that a series of READ operations must follow the record layout used when the data was written, and the types of variables must still be in one-to-one correspondence by type and ordering. And it is still possible to read partial records. The different data types are not interchangeable; one cannot WRITE with a FORMAT and later READ without one for example.

EXAMPLE: Data is prepared by

        DIMENSION A(5,5)
            :
            :
            :
        WRITE(63)A

which generates a single unformatted record of 25 real values. It can be read by

        REWIND 99
        READ(99)A

or part thereof. It *cannot* be replaced by 5 READ statements.

EXAMPLE: Data is prepared by

```
      DIMENSION A(5,5)
         :
         :
      DO 7Ø K=1,5
   7Ø WRITE(11)(A(K,L),L=1,5
```

It is in five records and can be read by

```
      REWIND(11)
      DO 91 K=1,5
   91 READ(11)(A(K,L),L=1,5)
```

As a final word to this section it is worth pointing out that FORTRAN does not automatically position a unit at a particular place at the beginning of a program. Particularly on a timesharing system it may be wise to REWIND units before processing; previous runs of the same or other programs during a session or a complicated processing job may have left the files not rewound.

8 The NAMELIST Facility

The NAMELIST statement provides an alternative means of reading data which is completely different from the FORMAT system. Although popular in some circles, it is little used in general. It appears to provide a simple means of presenting data to a program but in practice is rather troublesome. In a READ statement it is possible to put

READ(*n,name*)

where as usual *n* is a unit number and *name* is here the name given to a *list* of variables in a NAMELIST Statement

NAMELIST/*name*/*list*/$\frac{another}{name}$/$\frac{another}{list}$/... etc.

The NAMELIST statement must usually appear in the program before the READ. Using it, the *list* of variables desired by a READ statement is thus moved to a NAMELIST statement. No FORMAT is involved, and there are a few rules about what is allowed:

(i)   The *name* cannot be used anywhere else in the program, e.g. as variable name, function or subroutine name, or name of labelled common.

(ii) Variables can appear in several *lists* throughout the program.

The input data that is required in response to a READ instruction
using NAMELIST must be in a special form. The first character in
each record must be blank and the next one a special symbol, sometimes
$, sometimes &, followed without a break by the NAMELIST *name*. There-
fore the *name* occurs in the READ statement, the NAMELIST statement,
and in the data record itself. In the input data the *name* is followed
by a blank space and then items of data separated by commas. The items
of data continue in successive records until the group is ended by a
$END or &END signal.

The data in the input record consists of variable names and constants
equated to them, much like a string of simple arithmetic statements.
The data could be

> *variable name* = *constant* of the appropriate type. If
> LOGICAL use T or F

> *array variable name* = several *constants* of the appropriate
> type separated by commas. There should
> not be more than the array size. A
> constant repeated *k* times is expressed
> as *k*constant* much as in a DATA state-
> ment.

The order in which the *list* of variables is given by the data is
unimportant and this is the main attraction of the NAMELIST feature
along with the fact that the constant appears to be explicitly stated
as equated to a *variable name*.

EXAMPLE: A program contains:

>   NAMELIST/BLOG/X,Y,JOHN,MARY/
>   .
>   .
>   .
>   READ(5,BLOG)

Then to satisfy the READ statement, the data must give something
like

       $BLOG X=5.,Y=6.,JOHN=3,MARY=4$END

note the blanks before and after $BLOG. An extra comma after
MARY=4 could be used. The variables could be named in a different
order and several records could be given rather than just one. On
some computers read & for $.

If the program then contained

        WRITE(6,BLOG)

without the values altered in between then the output would be
  $BLOG

X=5.ØØ,Y=6.ØØ,JOHN=3,MARY=4

  $END

taking as many lines in general as would be necessary to provide
the data and with the beginning and ending messages on one line.

EXAMPLE: To read in a 5 x 5 unit matrix A:

        DIMENSION A(5,5)
              ⋮

        NAMELIST/MATRIX/A
              ⋮

        READ(5,MATRIX)

is in the program and the data could be

  $MATRIX A=1.,5*0.,1.,5*0.,1.,
  5*Ø.,1.,5*Ø.,1. $END

Index